CAPTAIN KHADOOS

ARJUN HEMMADY

TreeShade Books

Published by TreeShade Books (VB Performance LLP) in 2019

CAPTAIN KHADOOS

ISBN: 978-93-89237-07-8

Published by

TreeShade Books (VB Performance LLP)

Ansal Corporate Park, Sector142, Noida, Uttar Pradesh - 201305, India
Email - publish@TreeShadeBooks.com
www.TreeShadeBooks.com

Printed and Bound in India by
Thomson Press (India) Limited, 18/35 Delhi Mathura Road,
Faridabad – 121007 Haryana, India

Cover Illustration: The Book Bakers
Cover Design: Munisha Nanda
Typesetting: Ruchika Khanna

CAPTAIN KHADOOS

ARJUN HEMMADY

TreeShade Books
www.treeshadebooks.com

To my father, Late Dr. Sanjay Hemmady, the most influential person in my life. Miss you.

ACKNOWLEDGMENTS

I would like to take this opportunity to thank the people who have helped me in the journey of this book. I would like to express my gratitude to my literary agent, Suhail Mathur and his team at The Book Bakers, who had faith in me and my writing and for helping out with the cover design. I would like to thank Neil D'Silva, for whom I have the utmost admiration and respect for introducing me to Suhail. I would like to thank my publisher Vineet Bajpai of TreeShade Books for selecting my writing. My regards to Ruchika Khanna for guiding me through the entire publishing process. Also, I would like thank my editor, Harini Srinivasan for her valuable insights, tips and suggestions.

I would like to express my love to my entire family for their wholehearted support. In particular, my deep and heartfelt gratitude towards my father, Late Dr. Sanjay Hemmady, who, despite being terminally ill at that point in time, had gone through a rough draft of this story and appreciated it.

Lastly, but most importantly, I would like to thank my readers for reposing faith in me and reading my novel . I hope that you enjoy reading it as much as I enjoyed writing it.

AUTHOR'S NOTE

This novel has two themes – one of them is a sport that we love talking about and the other is a disease that we will do everything to avoid talking about: cricket and depression. Cricket is India's de facto national sport and we Indians can't get enough of it. Many of us may have thought of becoming cricketers at certain points in our lifetime. I know I certainly did. The attention, adulation and money which cricketers receive is something which has made cricket the most popular game in our country. And yes the fact that our National Team does pretty well more often than not also contributes to the tremendous viewership which the game generates. I still believe that despite the investment and encouragement being given to other sports, India still remains a country dominated by one sport i.e. cricket. There have been very few instances wherein we have collectively decided to stop watching the game. One of the moments that come to my mind is the World Cup in March/April, 2007 when the Indian cricket team was knocked out in the First Round. However, that phase did not last long as we once again pledged our unwavering devotion after the Indian cricket team won the T20 World Cup in September, 2007.

The second theme in this novel is about mental health, more specifically, depression. While we may think that people in our country have become more comfortable talking about depression, I would implore you to reconsider. There definitely has been a change in scenario in the past decade, when people slowly have become aware of what depression is . It has helped that celebrities have come out and openly talked about their struggles with this dreadful disease. However, there are two distinct concepts involved here – *awareness* and *acceptance*. While we may now be *aware* of depression, it seems to me that we are far away from *accepting* people with depression. I believe that it is still looked upon as a taboo to go to a psychologist or take psychiatric medicine. The notion that only "mad" people go to either of these practitioners is still prevalent.

Depression is not a disease that we choose to have. It is not a "sexy" disease. There was an article in a newspaper in 2018 which has stated that nearly half of India Inc employees suffer from depression. So why don't they speak up? I believe that it is because of lack of acceptance and understanding of the problem. People think that a person suffering from depression feels sad all the time. I disagree with this opinion. Depression is more complex than that. A sufferer of depression will show various symptoms some of which may include listlessness, a lack of hope, pessimism, over or under eating etc. It is important that the people who are in contact with such a person quickly recognise such signs and act swiftly and appropriately.

One must note that it is extremely difficult and to an extent, humiliating to admit to someone that one suffers from depression. The role of family, friends and colleagues is of utmost importance and it is vital that they know what they are doing when talking with the sufferers. They must be aware that such a person is in a vulnerable position. If you know anyone suffering from depression, I request you not to use comments like *"snap out of it"*, or *"it is just a phase, you will get over it"*, or *"why are you so mentally weak?"* or *"why are you so negative?"* The worst of them all however is, *"you have everything you need. Your body is functioning perfectly, look at people who have no arms or legs! Are they depressed?"* Such comments just increase the level of dejection and despair that the sufferer feels and it makes the person *feel bad about feeling bad* (it may sound strange, but it is actually a thing). Some people even shout at sufferers and humiliate them. Such acts should be strictly avoided. In extreme cases, bad advice is what makes a person take drastic decisions, one of which includes taking one's own life.

I have set this novel in the year 2025, wherein I hope that there will be much more *awareness* and *acceptance* about depression. I hope that there comes a day wherein we can openly talk about our mental health issues without the fear of being ridiculed, looked down upon or sidelined. There is a common misconception that people suffering from depression are mentally weak. **This is not true.** Depression does not discriminate. It can affect you regardless of your age, wealth or popularity. Some of the strongest men and women in the world have suffered from depression, one of whom is legendary American President Abraham Lincoln, who was known for having debilitating bouts of the disease, which in those days was called "melancholy".

What should one do when one is suffering from depression? I believe that one must accept it himself/herself. Self-acceptance is the first and most important step in **managing** the disease. However, this is where a lot of people get it wrong. In most cases, the sufferers are the last people to realise that they indeed are depressed. It is here that self-awareness and self-acceptance plays a huge part. One must be aware of one's normal behaviour and routines and should notice deviations from the same. Lack of appetite/excess appetite, lack/excess sleep, a feeling of worthlessness or helplessness and generally a sick feeling in the stomach are some of the numerous tell-tale signs. However, it must be noted that each person has different symptoms and the symptoms can't be generalised. But one must be careful also not to over-analyse oneself. Ups and downs are a part of everyone's life but one must start looking for help when such symptoms persist over a prolonged period of time.

It must be noted that a person suffering from depression will have his/her good moments also. That being said, it is common that sufferers will experience episodes ranging from delirious happiness to manic depression. Once again, it is important to realise it oneself when such episodes occur and not take any **life altering decisions**. It is easy and common to take impulsive decisions during such phases, but this is where one must be self-aware and talk to someone they trust about it. If they feel that the person they trust is unavailable at that particular moment, don't get dejected. Instead, one can pen down one's thoughts in a diary or notebook and go through the same after that delirious/depressive phase has passed away. We must realise that we are not our normal selves when we are going through phases like this and that decisions taken during these are usually impulsive and not well-thought out.

Now I come to the topic of treating depression. Should medication be taken or not? I believe that there is no right answer to it. However, one must not be averse to taking such psychiatric medication if it has been prescribed. Let me ask you a question. If you are diagnosed with diabetes and are prescribed insulin shots multiple times a day to maintain your blood sugar at healthy levels, will you take it or not? Most of the people will answer in the affirmative, because they realise that it is because our body is not producing the right amount of chemicals, an imbalance is being caused which is why we have been prescribed chemicals that will need to be consumed from an external source. And more often than not, a person taking insulin shots will not be ashamed of it and people who know him may, in fact, look at him as a source of inspiration as he is not allowing diabetes stop him from leading a healthy and normal life. So why is it that we have a different attitude when it comes to psychiatric medicines? Among other things, depression is also caused by chemical imbalances in our body and healthy levels of chemicals like serotonin can be maintained by taking medications.

Can depression be prevented? I wish I could answer in the affirmative. But life is long and there are no guarantees. That being said, it is recommended that a person with a history of depression should have a regular daily routine which he/she sticks to religiously as this leads them to **look forward to something.** However, there still is a chance that a person may suffer from depression once again even after following the routine diligently. Here, it is of vital importance to understand that this is **not a failure** on the part of the sufferer.

It is an inescapable fact that suffering from depression is uncomfortable. The notion that one will be prepared for it when it strikes the next time is half-baked at best. I always compare the discomfort suffered during depression to that of a boxer being punched during a bout. A boxer will put in thousands of hours of effort and training for the twelve rounds of a boxing match, but no matter how much he prepares, when he gets punched (which he will eventually), it is going to hurt the same. The difference between a seasoned boxer and a novice is that he will be prepared for the pain of the punch and will not panic. He will know what to do and what not to do in that situation.

Another question people ask is should one meditate during depression? I have myself interacted with people who have claimed that they have cured themselves from the disease without medication by meditation. I will humbly disagree with such people. According to my understanding, meditation is the art of focussing one's mind on one thing only. I believe that can be done only when one has the ideal conditions to do so. In my opinion, a person with depression is not in an ideal state of mind to meditate because thousands of uncontrolled thoughts are moving through his/her head making it close to impossible to focus on one thing. Just like we will get the best results for growing crops when we have fertile soil, adequate fertilisers and abundant water supply, similarly, a stable and uncluttered mind is best suited for meditation.

To conclude, I will ask one question – what must a person with a history of suffering from depression aspire for? I believe that such a person must have realistic ambitions from life and must aspire for emotional stability. The Sanskrit term called *Stithpragya* or the process of maintaining equilibrium should be aspired for. This means that while there will be mood swings, they will not be major and instead of acting impulsively during such phases, we will understand it and let that phase pass. Thoughts will come. It is in the nature of the mind to distract us. The mind is like a monkey, always jumping from one place to another, never staying still, always restless. It is vital that we understand this. Depression is a disease that is **managed** and **not fought**. If one goes into the situation with the intention of fighting, then the whole process becomes toxic. Instead, one must be tactful and self-aware. We are all unique and must not compare ourselves with others. If we want to compare ourselves at all with anyone, we should do so with past versions of ourselves. No matter what anyone says, one must **never ever be ashamed** of suffering from depression. Instead one must look at oneself as a source of inspiration. We should pat ourselves on the back that we have not given up. The mere fact that one gets up in the morning, does his/her daily chores and goes to work diligently is something one must be extremely proud of. We are heroes. We are champions. Don't let anyone let you think otherwise.

I AM HUMAN TOO

"This is not right," mumbled Suraj to himself.

"What's the matter?" asked his friend, Aditi.

"Look at this," said Suraj and showed her the article in the newspaper, "they are making a joke out of him. So what if he decided to take a break to deal with his mental health issues! People take breaks all the time to deal with their physical health issues! We are in 2027, for God's sake. Why are people still so immature?"

"Everybody has not gone through what you have."

"Should I tell you the statistics of the number of people who suffer from depression in India? I can quote those numbers even in my sleep."

"I know the numbers, Suraj," she replied, "I am a psychologist; I have to know these numbers."

"Somebody has to do something about it," grumbled Suraj, as they sat in a coffee shop at Girgaum Chowpatty, a locality in Mumbai.

"Why don't you do something?"

"Like what?"

"Why don't you give an interview?"

"Hmm, I'm not good at giving interviews."

"I think people will really appreciate it coming from you."

"You think?"

"Why not? You are the captain of the Indian Cricket Team! Coming from you, people will listen to what you have to say."

"Really? Coming out in the open talking about my depression doesn't seem like a good idea," said Suraj, a frown on his face. "I'd rather tell the world that I am gay than depressed. They will at least accept that. If I tell them that I had depression, they will say *so what? He's feeling a little sad, tell him to get over it!*"

"Oh come on, people are not so stupid now."

"Trust me Aditi, they are."

"Okay, will you do something for me?"

"Yeah, sure, anything," said Suraj eagerly.

"Tell your agent to call up any news channel and tell them that you have an announcement to make," she said. "But don't tell them what the announcement is. Let them speculate and lose their mind for a few days."

"Okay, if you say so," he said, "but to let you know, I'm not convinced. People in our country are still not ready to accept that it's okay to go to a psychologist or take psychiatric medication. And I don't know if my giving such an interview will convince anybody."

"Should I quote that verse from the Gita again?" asked Aditi.

"No, it's okay. I know it," replied Suraj. "Y*ou have control over your actions, but not on the fruit of your actions*."

"*And if you don't succeed, don't succumb to inactivity,*" she said.

THE RIPPLE EFFECT

Suraj's first televised interview sent shockwaves through the length and breadth of the country.

"I have suffered from depression and have taken medication for it. No, I am not ashamed. In fact, I am still on medication for it." News channels kept playing these lines again and again.

"Why don't you snap out of it?" was one of the questions that the interviewer asked Suraj.

"Do you tell a person who suffers from heart disease or diabetes to snap out of it?" shot back Suraj.

"But those are diseases of the body," said the interviewer.

"The brain is also part of the body isn't it?" replied Suraj. "Why do we look at people differently just because they have some problem *up here*? Just like the body, the mind also gets sick from time to time, and some people have a greater tendency to get depressed when compared to others."

A couple of days after the interview, Suraj parked his car in the basement of his father's apartment in Girgaum. The apartment was a couple of kilometres away from the seashore in Mumbai. Suraj had purchased a flat from the earnings of his first IPL contract and had moved out from his childhood home.

He rang the bell and waited. A couple of moments later, a tall middle-aged man who still looked fairly young opened the door.

"Come in Suraj," said Suraj's father, Sanjeev.

"Hi Papa," said Suraj.

"So, how are you doing?" asked his father as they sat down in the living room.

"Fine," replied Suraj.

"I saw your interview," said Sanjeev, getting right to the point.

"Hmm," replied Suraj, "what did you think of it?"

"Well, it was good," he replied.

"Okay," replied Suraj.

"You know that you have painted a huge target on your back right? The Australians must have watched it. Don't you think they will use it to their advantage?" said Sanjeev.

"I don't care what they think," said Suraj. "I had to take a stand."

"But couldn't you take the stand some other time?" asked Sanjeev.

"Like when?" asked Suraj.

"I don't know," replied Sanjeev, "like maybe the day you retired?"

"Oh come on Papa," said Suraj, feeling dejected, "can't you agree with what I have done just this one time? You saw the way the media made a joke of that CEO didn't you?"

"I did," replied Sanjeev, "but there are other ways of showing your support. By saying that you suffer from mental illness, you have not only damaged your own reputation, but have also jeopardised the performance and well-being of your team."

"Okay, but everybody is saying that it is a step in the right direction," explained Suraj.

"I don't care what everybody else says," said back his father. "Seriously, I can't for the life of me understand why you fall for this flattery every damn time."

"What flattery? There is a difference between flattery and praise," said Suraj, his voice rising.

"Mind your tone, young man," snapped Sanjeev.

Suraj became quiet, as he felt humiliated and leaned back in the chair.

This was one of the reasons why he had moved out of the apartment in which he had spent his childhood. Suraj's mother had passed away when he was an infant and his father was the person who had brought him up. But he was a hard man, tough to impress and he rarely praised Suraj.

After an uneasy silence, Suraj got up and walked towards the door.

"Bye Papa," said Suraj.

"When will I see you again?" asked Sanjeev.

"I don't know," replied Suraj, "maybe after coming back from Australia."

"Okay, then all the best," said Sanjeev.

"Oh come on Papa, we both know that you don't mean that," snorted Suraj and walked out of the door.

When Suraj sat in his car, he put his head back, leaning into the headrest and closed his eyes. *What would it take for him to get his father's approval?* He thought to himself.

CONFUSION, CONFUSION, CONFUSION

Suraj checked his bag one last time to see whether he had packed everything he needed for the three month long Tour of Australia.

"Shall we leave?" asked Aditi, who was standing by the door, impatiently looking at her wristwatch.

"Yeah, let's go," replied Suraj and closed the bags.

The two of them placed the bags in the trunk of Aditi's car. It was a tradition that Aditi would have dinner with Suraj and drop him off at the airport on the night of his departure for a Tour. They went to Aditi's favourite restaurant and post dinner, made their way towards the airport.

Aditi had estimated that it would take them at least an hour to reach the airport from the restaurant, but to their pleasant surprise the drive took much less time than expected. When they reached the airport, there were still three hours left for Suraj's flight to take off. They parked the car in the airport parking terminal and decided to have a cup of coffee. The next two hours were spent chatting – with Suraj feeling the most relaxed he had felt in a long time.

Aditi on the other hand had a lump in her throat. She would not see Suraj for the next three months, and that made her sad.

"Why can't I come with you on the tour?"

"Because wives and girlfriends are not allowed on tour."

"But I am neither your wife nor your girlfriend."

"It's not that easy."

"How about if you say that I am your personal psychologist?"

"We already have a team Psychologist."

"Okay," she replied.

"Come on," said Suraj after a few moments and got up, "I think I had better make a move."

"Okay," replied Aditi, trying to mask the sadness she was feeling.

When they reached the Departure Lounge, Aditi felt her emotions reach a crescendo.

"Wait, Suraj," she said and held his hand.

"What?" he asked and turned around.

"I want to tell you something," said Aditi.

"Okay, what is it?" asked Suraj. "Tell me quickly because I have to leave."

"It's just that," said Aditi, feeling tears run down her cheeks, "I'll miss you a lot Suraj."

"I'll miss you too," replied Suraj and gave her a tight hug.

Aditi hugged him back and hoped that the moment would never pass. When they let go, Aditi took Suraj's face into her hands and touched her lips to his.

"What are you doing?" asked a shocked Suraj.

"I think I love you Suraj," blurted out Aditi.

"What?" said Suraj, at a loss for words.

"I wanted to tell you a few days ago," said Aditi, between sobs, "but I didn't know how to tell you."

"Okay," replied Suraj, not knowing what to say.

"So, do you also have feelings for me?" asked Aditi.

Suraj stood transfixed at the spot. He felt a chill down his spine, and thought how he could extricate himself from that uncomfortable moment. He definitely liked Aditi as a friend, but he wasn't sure he had romantic feelings for her.

"Suraj!" said Aditi, with urgency in her voice. "Do you have feelings for me?"

"Listen Aditi," said a surprised Suraj who put his hands on her shoulders in an attempt to calm her. "I think you are awesome, but-"

"Oh, here comes the *but*," said Aditi, feeling dejected. "Is it a yes or a no?"

"What do you want me to say Aditi?" said Suraj.

"It's so simple dammit, do you like me or not?" she asked him again.

"Uh, I don't know if I like you or not," replied Suraj.

"Screw this, I'm going home," replied Aditi and walked away in a huff.

"Aditi, wait!" exclaimed Suraj loudly, but to no avail.

Aditi left the place as quickly as she could. Suraj cursed himself for behaving in such an indecisive way.

As Suraj boarded the airplane, he had a sick feeling in his stomach. *Did he like Aditi?* He wasn't sure of the answer himself. "*We do spend a lot of time together even though we are not romantically involved with each other. But why did she have to bring that up now, just before this tour? She knows how hard I have worked for this tournament,*" Suraj thought as he sat on his designated seat in the First Class Cabin of the Airbus A380. He closed his eyes and hoped that he would be rested and that his mind would be clearer when he woke up.

THE PAST

THE SCHOOL TEAM

Lunch break at St. Mary's ICSE School in Mazgaon, Mumbai.

Suraj, an eighth standard student, was sitting at the edge of the large ground next to the basketball court. As he sat looking around, he saw a red rubber ball coming towards him. He picked up the ball.

"Hey give us the ball sonny!" said a boy who walked up to Suraj.

"Just a minute," replied Suraj and walked towards where the boys were playing cricket.

"Can't you hear? Are you deaf or something?" said the boy aggressively, "I said give me the ball!"

"Wait a minute!" replied Suraj assertively.

The rest of the boys playing the game stopped to look at the tall, well-built boy who was walking towards them. Suraj stopped walking a few feet before the makeshift stumps, tiffin boxes placed next to each other.

"What are you doing?" asked the boy.

"Tell him to bat," replied Suraj.

"But you are not playing with us," said the boy.

"Just do as I say," said Suraj firmly.

When the boy with the bat took guard, Suraj started running towards the tiffin boxes and bowled a delivery. Before the boy could react, the ball had beaten his bat and had hit the wall behind him. He had been bowled.

The entire group was stunned.

"What the fuck did you just do?" asked the boy who was batting.

"I just bowled a ball," replied Suraj with a shrug.

"Can you do it again?"

"I guess I can," said Suraj.

"Hey but don't we have a game to finish!" said the other boys as Suraj walked past the tiffin boxes.

"Just wait and watch this guy," said the boy who was batting, "he is the fastest bowler I have ever faced."

Suraj bowled another six balls at the boy.

"Okay, that's enough," said the boy and walked towards Suraj, "what's your name kid?"

"Suraj," replied Suraj, "what's your name?"

"My name is Varun, I am the school cricket captain." replied the boy. "Which grade are you in?"

"Eighth," replied Suraj.

"Have you played cricket before?" he asked.

"No," was the reply.

"Hmm," said Varun, "come to school tomorrow at seven in the morning."

"Why?" asked Suraj.

"Because I'll get you into the school cricket team," replied Varun.

The next morning, Suraj, in a pair of track pants and a t-shirt, reached the school grounds at 6:45 am.

Varun was already there and was talking to the coach, Mr. D'Mello, a middle-aged man of average height.

"Is this the kid you were talking about?" asked Mr. D'Mello.

"Yes, Sir," replied Varun, "honestly, he is the fastest bowler I have ever faced."

"Hmm, but I'll still have to test him," said Mr. D'Mello.

"Yes, Sir, I understand," replied Varun.

Suraj walked up to the two of them and exchanged pleasantries.

"Have you played cricket before?" asked Mr. D'Mello.

"No," was Suraj's short reply.

"Hmm," said the coach. "Okay, that won't be a problem. Now start warming up. Varun, show him some exercises."

"Come here Suraj," said Varun, "let's start with some stretches. After that we will run five laps around the ground."

"Five laps?" asked Suraj, sounding worried.

"Yes," replied Varun, "you are a fast bowler, so you must have good stamina."

"But I've never even run one lap around the ground," said Suraj.

"There's always a first time for everything right?" replied Varun with a chuckle as he started stretching.

Suraj was out of breath after just one lap, but with Varun's encouragement, he managed to complete the five laps. After running, they started practicing catching. The bowlers of the squad were then given a go to bowl to the batsmen.

"Suraj, you're next," said Mr. D'Mello and threw the ball to him.

Suraj took his run up and bowled a ball which landed at good length and was dispatched easily by the batsman. Suraj bowled for about fifteen minutes after which he said that he had had enough.

"Okay, have some water," said Mr. D'Mello and walked towards Varun.

"What do you think, coach?" asked Varun, expectantly.

"He's fast, that is for sure," replied Mr. D'Mello.

"But what?" asked Varun, knowing that Mr. D'Mello had something on his mind.

"There is no consistency," said the coach, a frown on his face, "he's wayward."

"But we can work on that right?" asked Varun.

"Yes, but it'll take a lot of work," replied Mr. D'Mello.

"Don't worry Sir. That will be my responsibility," said Varun, "I'll see to it that he gets as much practice as he possibly can."

"Okay," he replied, "that's fine with me."

For the next few months, Varun saw to it that Suraj bowled as much as possible. He even called him on weekends to play with his friends. During these practice sessions, Varun observed that Suraj was also a capable batsman even though his technique and batting style was very unorthodox. He also realized that Suraj was unsure of himself and needed constant encouragement.

"He'll have to toughen up mentally, if he wants to make a career out of cricket," said Mr. D'Mello to Varun one day after practice.

"Yes Sir, I agree," replied Varun.

"What can we do about his batting technique?" said Mr. D'Mello, sounding irritated. "He holds the bat all wrong, his stance is strange and he's always fidgeting when he is about to face the ball."

"Yes, but he's scoring runs, isn't he?" suggested Varun.

"He is scoring runs, I'm not denying that," said Mr. D'Mello. "One day he may also be a good batsman, but the point is that for succeeding at a higher level, he needs to have a sound technique and that's what is missing in him. Sometimes I wonder if it's too late to correct it. And keep this in mind Varun, this kid has potential."

"You mean he can play in the school team?" asked Varun.

"No, I mean he can play for India," replied Mr. D'Mello.

TECHNIQUE IS HIGHLY OVERRATED

A few days later, during a practice session, Mr. D'Mello, who had been observing the players intently, decided to suggest changes in Suraj's batting technique.

"Not like that Suraj!" said Mr. D'Mello irritably.

"What happened Sir?" asked Suraj.

"Come here."

"Yes Sir?"

"You must change your batting technique."

"Okay Sir."

"Now do as I say," said Mr. D'Mello showing him the classical stance of a batsman, "now that's good. When you have a side on stance, you can play on both sides of the wicket."

"Okay Sir," said Suraj following his coach's instructions.

"Now the first inter-school match is taking place next week. I want you to practice with Varun and get your technique right."

"Okay Sir."

"Varun! Come here!" called out Mr. D'Mello.

"Yes Sir?" asked Varun when he came close to them.

"Give Suraj some batting practice and see to it that he uses a proper and orthodox technique," said Mr. D'Mello.

"Sure Sir," said Varun and walked away with Suraj.

But adjusting to the new technique was not easy for Suraj. He was used to having an open stance with his chest facing the bowler and his bat placed between his feet. A technically correct batsman would have a side on stance with his chest facing away from the bowler and his bat placed behind his back foot. Usually, left-handed batsmen with a correct stance were famous for their impeccable timing. This led to the reputation of them being elegant. However, Suraj, while a left-handed batsman was the complete antithesis to this. As he was a well-built boy, power was an important part of his game but his repertoire of shots was limited. An open stance meant that he was not able to play the cover drive effectively and his straight drive would inevitably wind up going towards mid-on, instead of straight down the ground. And this irritated Mr. D'Mello to no end. This was why he was insisting on changing Suraj's batting style.

After a lot of hard work, Suraj managed to make his batting look more correct. But the results were not coming. Suraj got out cheaply in every match in the inter-school tournament. He was sent to bat at No. 7, an important position and a link between the middle and lower order. But with Suraj not contributing with the bat, it was left to the bowlers to save the day in most matches. Thankfully, Suraj was lethal with the ball. He had learnt to swing the ball prodigiously and that was something which made the opposition teams dread his bowling. But the lack of results with the bat was a cause of concern for his team. Realising that something was not right, Mr. D'Mello decided to talk to Suraj.

"Suraj, is anything bothering you?" asked Mr. D'Mello, one day before they started their practice.

"No Sir," replied Suraj, "everything is fine."

"Then why are you not scoring runs?" he asked.

"I don't know," replied Suraj evasively.

"Are you having trouble adjusting to the new technique?" asked Mr. D'Mello.

"No Sir," replied Suraj.

"Listen Suraj, if you think that the new batting technique is causing you problems, then you can go back to your natural batting stance," suggested Mr. D'Mello.

"Are you sure, Sir?" asked Suraj, feeling expectant.

"Yes Suraj, I'm positive," said his coach.

"Thanks Sir," replied Suraj with a smile.

A little later when the team was practising, Varun was surprised to see Suraj batting with his earlier stance.

Varun walked up to Mr. D'Mello and asked, "Sir, why is Suraj batting like this? Had you not told him to change his technique?"

"Yeah, I had," replied the coach.

"Then why has he gone back to his earlier stance?" asked Varun.

"You know, sometimes technique is highly overrated," said Mr. D'Mello with a chuckle. "I always thought that a good technique is required to deal with hostile bowling. But Suraj has proved me wrong. More than a good technique, it is important to know how to utilise your available talent and ability to the fullest."

"Hmm," said Varun, surprised that a stickler for batting techniques such as Mr. D'Mello had relented and allowed Suraj to go back to his original batting style.

The change in technique did wonders and Suraj started scoring runs again. Suraj became unstoppable with both bat and ball in the latter part of the ongoing tournaments. It was on one of those days that Suraj was promoted to opening the batting. That day he scored a century.

MAKING HIS MARK

Years passed by. Suraj made waves in the cricket circuit. By the age of 19, Suraj was in the Mumbai cricket team and within two years, he made his debut for the Indian cricket team. Suraj's bowling took the entire nation by storm. Suraj was the bowler that India so desperately needed. He had lethal swing and could bowl at speeds in excess of 150 kmph. However his batting was overlooked as he was constantly made to play at No. 9 or 10 despite his protests that he was a capable batsman.

It was during the India versus New Zealand Test Series in 2021 that this changed.

In the third and final test match that took place at the Eden Gardens in Kolkata, India slumped to 53 for 7 in reply to New Zealand's score of 354 on a seaming wicket. At this stage, Suraj walked out to bat.

"Hang in there," said Vikrant, the captain of the team who was batting, "the ball is swinging a lot. Play sensibly."

"Sure," replied Suraj bumping fists with his captain.

Suraj looked around the ground and smiled. The stands at Eden Gardens were filled to the brim. The time had come for him to prove that he could indeed bat.

Suraj asked the umpire to give him a middle stump guard, and marked the line with his shoe. After removing a bail from over the stumps, he banged it into the ground to make a permanent mark.

But the going was difficult. The Kiwi bowlers cranked up the pace and bowled beautiful swinging deliveries that made life challenging for Suraj and Vikrant out in the middle.

Even after a few hours, Suraj's score was only 26 runs of 169 balls. But he was not worried. He was determined to take his team out of danger no matter how long it took. Suraj got behind the line of each and every delivery and played it at the last moment dealing with the late swing which the New Zealand bowlers were generating.

And the plan worked. Before he knew it, he had scored his first half century in test cricket. The entire 60,000 strong crowd at the Eden Gardens got onto their feet to applaud Suraj's gutsy knock. But his job was only half complete. Suraj intended to make such a mark with the bat that he would never be told to bat lower down the order again.

He felt a tingle of excitement as he neared the three figure mark. However, a century wasn't to be, as the last 3 wickets fell in a space of 11 balls as Suraj was left stranded with his score at 96 runs off 363 balls.

Feeling dejected, he punched his bat with his gloves and walked off the field, oblivious to the applause of the crowd, the New Zealand team and the Indian contingent back in the dressing room.

"Awesome job Suraj!" said everyone in the dressing room as they congratulated him for an amazing knock of 96 runs. Suraj smiled at everyone, but deep inside he knew that the century had been his for the taking.

A few days later, during the first One Day International against the New Zealanders, Suraj was promoted up the batting order. Batting at number 3, he didn't disappoint and scored an imperious knock of 74 runs to win India the match. It seemed then that India's eternal search for an all-rounder who could bowl fast had ended.

THE BLACK DOG

For the next two years, Suraj performed consistently with both bat and ball. He was constantly either playing or practicing. This led to many injuries. He also did not miss any matches and ignored the usual aches and pains that he would feel. He would continue to play and ignore the discomfort by taking painkillers. To an outsider it seemed that he had everything going well for him in his life, but inside his mind, something was amiss.

He started experiencing mood swings and oscillated between episodes of extreme happiness and sadness. There would be days when he would feel that he had nothing to look forward to. Suraj thought that this would all pass away after a few days and did not know what to do. He tried talking with his father about it, but that talk did more harm than good.

The only respite Suraj found was in food. He was truly happy when eating and therefore he started eating huge amounts of food to cope with his swinging emotions.

A tour to Australia had been planned for December 2023 and the team management wanted Suraj to be at his best for that. So they instructed him to skip an upcoming series against the West Indies; they wanted him to recharge his batteries. However, instead of dealing with his emotions, Suraj stopped training for the duration of his break and focussed only on eating.

By the time he rejoined the Indian team before the First Test in Adelaide, Suraj had gained a significant amount of weight. The Australian commentators sniggered when they saw a clearly overweight Suraj lumber towards the crease for his run up.

The lack of fitness was evident as Suraj strained a hamstring muscle in his second spell of the day. This led to Suraj feeling even more helpless and this did not escape the attention of the physiotherapist of the Indian Team. He had a long talk with Suraj and told him that he was going through severe depression. His suggestion was that Suraj go back to India and deal with the issue by consulting a psychologist.

"A psychologist? But I am not mad!" protested Suraj when he heard the suggestion.

"I know you are not mad, Suraj," he said. "But it is important to deal with this before it gets out of hand."

"Who should I meet? I don't know any psychologist, I've never been to one," said Suraj.

"Don't worry," he said. "Now tell me, will you be more comfortable talking to a man or a woman?"

"Would it make a difference?" asked Suraj.

"Actually," he explained, "it is just that some people find it easier to open to the same sex."

"I'm okay with anyone I guess," said Suraj with a shrug of his shoulders.

"Then I have just the guy for you," he said and gave him a phone number.

"Dr. Kulkarni," said Suraj looking at the name above the number.

"He's a psychiatrist," he said, "and he works with his daughter Aditi who is a psychologist."

Later that evening Suraj called up that number and fixed an appointment for a day later in the week and flew back to India.

THE FIRST MEETING

Dr. Kulkarni was a man in his early sixties with a wicked sense of humour. His daughter Aditi, in her late twenties, was more reserved. They worked in tandem from their clinic in Opera House, in Mumbai with Suraj having a consult with Aditi first and then her father to work out the dosage of the medicines.

Suraj and Aditi hit it off at once. He felt he could trust her and did not hold back from divulging even the most embarrassing details or events. He also learnt that she was an avid cricket fan and had followed his career very closely. "*That knock against New Zealand was epic*", she commented in one of their sessions.

After a few sessions, Aditi and her father ascertained that Suraj's issues were partly due to his difficult relationship with his father. Hypnosis sessions were also conducted to explore further into his personality. The sessions revealed that Suraj had a deep sense of inadequateness. Aditi assured Suraj that they would work on those issues after resolving his current problem.

Slowly, but surely, Suraj improved and was able to get out of his depressive phase. However, his life otherwise was in shambles. His habit of eating heavily still persisted and since he was not training, he gained even more weight.

One day after a session, Suraj and Aditi went for lunch. It was then that Aditi noticed Suraj's eating habits and realised that he indeed had an unhealthy attachment to eating.

"What do you want out of your life, Suraj?" she asked him after they had finished their meal.

"I don't know," replied Suraj with a shrug, "I'm just taking it one day at a time."

"That's nice," she replied, "but at the same time you must also have a long term plan in your mind."

"Okay," he replied.

"Suraj, I want you to do something for me," said Aditi, after a while.

"Sure," replied Suraj, "what can I do?"

"I want you to get back into the Indian Cricket team," she said.

"Okay," he replied, "but didn't you say that I should focus on getting better now?"

"You are much better, Suraj," she said. "I see huge potential in you, don't waste it."

"But I was thinking of going back to studies and getting an MBA or something," said Suraj.

"No, you must get back into the Indian Cricket team," she said firmly. "We can work out a plan together if you want."

"Sure," replied Suraj after a moment, "I'd like that."

They then went back to Aditi's office and drew up a plan of action. They noted down everything that Suraj needed to do to get back into the Indian team within the next one year.

"You have my total support Suraj," said Aditi after handing him over a paper with the details, "if you have any queries or doubts, don't hesitate to ping or call me."

WEIGHTY ISSUES

After the honest talk with Aditi, Suraj found himself in deep thought. He knew that he had to do something to get his life back on track. Looking at himself in the mirror, particularly at his midriff, it was clear that he was out of shape. When he weighed himself on the weighing scales, he realised that he was some 16 kilograms overweight. The scales showed that he weighed 98.5 kilograms. For Suraj's height of six feet two and a half inches, the ideal weight should have been around 82 kilograms.

Suraj knew that he had to make a change. He made up his mind that he would now get his life back on track. He noted that the Ranji Trophy season was to start in six months - enough time for him to get back into shape. It had also been a few months since he had last bowled and he knew that he needed practice. Looking and feeling physically fit was not enough. He had to be in good form while playing the game also if he had any chance of being selected for the Mumbai Ranji Team. He spoke to the coach of the Mumbai cricket Team and informed him that he would like to participate in the next season of the Ranji trophy. The coach asked him to come to the Wankhede stadium the next day.

The next morning, Suraj went for a long jog upon waking up, followed by a healthy breakfast. He then made his way towards the Wankhede stadium, where he hesitatingly walked up to meet the coach, Mr. Mazumdar.

"Hello Sir," said Suraj.

"How can I help you, Suraj?" asked Mr. Mazumdar.

"I want to play again, Sir," said Suraj.

"Why?" he asked, "I heard that you had quit."

"I have changed my mind now," replied Suraj.

"Oh yeah? What if you change your mind again tomorrow?" said Mr. Mazumdar. "I don't have time for you if you keep on changing your mind everyday Suraj."

"I won't change my mind, Sir," said Suraj, "I have promised a friend that I will play for India again."

"Hmm," said the coach thoughtfully. "You can start tomorrow."

"Thank you Sir," said Suraj feeling relieved, "I won't let you down."

"Don't worry about me Suraj," he said, "don't let yourself down."

GOT TO TRY AGAIN

The euphoria and excitement which Suraj felt after topping the batting and bowling Averages in the recently concluded Ranji Trophy season was soon replaced by a sense of dejection. Suraj had thought that his selection in the Team would be a formality after his stellar performances. But he was not among the players who were selected for the Tour of Sri Lanka. Feeling sick in his stomach, he once again went through the names in the list hoping that he had missed reading his name. But there was no change. The sense of helplessness rose by the second. Several players had been given a second chance to redeem themselves and a couple of new players had been included in the squad.

How could they have left me out? Suraj just could not understand. He had pushed himself to the limit the past few months to regain his form and fitness. He called Aditi and confided in her. He poured out his feeling of helplessness. She reassured him saying that while he had done everything he could at the time, he must also think about what was missing.

After the phone call, Suraj got an idea and he dialed the number of Mr. Mazumdar.

"Hello Sir, Suraj here."

"Yes, Suraj," replied Mr. Mazumdar, "how can I help you?"

"Can I meet you?" asked Suraj.

"Yeah, sure," he said, "when do you want to meet?"

"Are you free now?" asked Suraj.

"Yes," he replied, "come to the Gymkhana, I'll be there."

"Thank you Sir," said Suraj and hung up.

About half an hour later, Suraj sat in the air conditioned room in Hindu Gymkhana at Marine Drive along with the Coach of the Mumbai Ranji Team.

"Hello Sir," said Suraj.

"Yes Suraj. How are you?" asked Mr. Mazumdar.

"The Team for the Sri Lanka Tour was declared today," said Suraj.

"Yes, I know," replied the Coach.

"I thought that I would be selected," said Suraj, "I topped the batting and bowling averages. What else do the selectors want me to do?"

"See Suraj, I don't know what went on in the minds of the selectors," he said. "But there is one thing."

"What's that?" asked Suraj.

"You are not a complete player," said the Coach.

"Pardon me?" said Suraj, feeling offended.

"Ask yourself Suraj, can you bowl an outswinger? Can you do reverse swing?" asked Mr. Mazumdar.

"I can do an out swing with a new ball," said Suraj, still feeling incensed.

"Oh come on, any fast bowler worth his salt can do that," he said. "The question is can you swing the old ball? Huh? Can you make the batsmen dance to your tunes when the ball has lost its shine?"

"I've never tried it," admitted Suraj.

"*That's* what is missing," he said forcefully.

"So what should I do?" asked Suraj. "The next season doesn't start for a few months."

"You can go to England," he suggested. "I can put in a good word if you want."

"England? To play County cricket?" asked Suraj, feeling apprehensive.

"Yes," said the Coach. "Over there you will play cricket day in and day out. And if you are not good enough, you will be dropped for sure. If you decide to play in England, you must constantly be on your toes, sharpening your skills."

"But from whom can I learn to bowl reverse swing, or swinging the old ball?" asked Suraj.

"There is a person who can help you with that," said the Coach and leaned forward.

"Okay, who is it?" asked Suraj, his curiosity peaking.

"Mehul Patel," said the Coach.

"Mehul? You mean that guy who used to play for Baroda?" said Suraj.

"Yes," said the Coach. "He is settled in England now. He's a good friend of mine and he's always ready to take a promising cricketer under his wing."

"But why do you think he'll help me?" asked Suraj warily.

"Because he's very impressed by your bowling," said the Coach.

"So is Mehul going to play this County season?" asked Suraj.

"Oh yes, he plays every County season without fail," replied Mr. Mazumdar.

"How should I go about it?" asked Suraj.

"I'll tell you," he said. "But first tell me, are you ready to go England and stay there for six months and play nonstop cricket?"

Suraj thought for a while. He accepted that he had to do something different. Mr. Mazumdar was right. Suraj did depend too much on his inswinger and after a point in time it was easy for the batsmen to pick it. He was successful in the Ranji Trophy mainly because very few batsmen were used to facing anybody with Suraj's speed. Suraj's pace instilled fear in batsmen in the domestic arena, but speed wouldn't be his friend in international cricket where the batsmen were more skilled and battle-hardened.

"Yes, I am ready," said Suraj after weighing pros and cons.

"Are you sure? Don't bail out at the last minute," said the Coach.

"No, I won't," replied Suraj.

"Okay, then," said the Coach, "I'll make the calls and get you on a plane to Yorkshire."

SWINGING IT BOTH WAYS

"What did you want to talk about?" asked Mehul to Suraj, a few days after he arrived in Yorkshire.

"Uh, I want to learn reverse swing," said Suraj reluctantly.

"Hmm," replied the 37-year-old supremely fit all rounder from Baroda, "I was wondering when you would ask me that."

"So will you teach me?" asked Suraj.

"I have no problem teaching you," he replied, "but are you willing to learn?"

"What do you mean?" asked Suraj.

"Are you willing to re-learn everything about bowling?" asked Mehul. "I had a word with Mazumdar. I discussed a lot of things with him. One of the problems you had was that you did not receive good coaching early on in your career."

"Excuse me?" said Suraj feeling slighted.

"See Suraj," explained Mehul, "this is what I am talking about. I have lot of regard for Mazumdar and I have also heard about your school team's coach. But even though both of them are good coaches, they are batsmen. And batsmen usually don't know much about the intricacies of bowling. I hope you don't misunderstand me. It is commendable that you have reached this far in international cricket. But to take your game to the next level, you must do as I say."

"Yes, I'll do as you say," said Suraj.

"Good," replied Mehul. "I'll see you in the indoor stadium at 5 am tomorrow morning."

"5 am?" said Suraj in shock.

"Do you want to learn or not?" asked Mehul.

"Yes," replied Suraj.

"Then you will meet me at 5 am tomorrow morning, I will make the necessary arrangements," said Mehul.

The next morning Suraj woke up at 4:50 am, got dressed and reached the stadium. To his surprise, Mehul was already there and was doing some stretching. Suraj picked up a red cricket ball which was lying on the ground and walked up to his County Teammate.

"So, how do you do reverse swing?" asked Suraj, getting straight to the point.

"We'll talk about that later," replied Mehul and took the ball from Suraj's hand, "first let's do some running on the treadmill."

"But how will that help me to learn reverse swing?" asked Suraj.

"You'll get to know in some time," was Mehul's short reply.

The two of them went on the treadmill in the empty gym and ran for eight kilometers. They followed this by leg exercises. After two hours of strenuous physical activity, Suraj was completely exhausted. When they walked to the pitch in the indoor stadium, it was clear that Suraj was functioning on reserve energy.

"Now bowl ten overs at me," instructed Mehul.

"But-" started Suraj.

"I'll tell you why I am doing all this," said Mehul patiently, "but for now just do as I say."

Suraj did as he was told and bowled ten overs to Mehul. At the end of the ten overs, Suraj lay down on the floor, completely drained of all energy.

"Come on get up!" urged Mehul, "you wanted to learn reverse swing didn't you? Now get up!"

"I can't!" said Suraj and lay on his back, panting.

"Do you know why I made you do all this?" asked Mehul.

"I haven't the foggiest," replied Suraj, closing his eyes.

"I made you do this because the ball starts reversing towards the end of the day," explained Mehul, "and by that time you will be as tired as you are right now. Doing reverse swing requires not only skill, but also strength and fitness. It takes extra effort to make the ball do something which it is not normally meant to do."

"So why didn't you tell me all this before?" asked Suraj, and sat up.

"Because I wanted to test you," replied Mehul.

"And did I pass?" he asked.

"With flying colours," replied Mehul, "you have done better than anyone I have taught."

"Thanks," replied Suraj with a grin.

"Now get up," said Mehul, "you are only half-way through. I have not yet taught you the correct wrist position for doing swing bowling."

"But I know it already," protested Suraj, not wanting to learn something he already knew.

"Your wrist position is wrong, Suraj," explained Mehul, "your wrist must be behind the ball so that when you release it, it lands on the seam. The ball should not wobble in the air; it has to fall straight on the seam."

"So does the ball wobble when I bowl?" asked Suraj, hoping to get a compliment from the great fast bowler and all-rounder who had one of the most prolific records in Indian domestic cricket.

"Yes," replied Mehul, "it wobbles a lot."

"Okay," replied Suraj, dejected, "how should I stop it from wobbling?"

"Come here, I'll show you," said Mehul and beckoned Suraj towards him.

That was their schedule for the remainder of the County Season. They woke up at 5 am every morning no matter how much their bodies hurt and pushed themselves to the limit. Suraj ended the County season by being one of the top five wicket takers that year.

"Now am I ready?" asked Suraj to Mehul on the last day of the Season.

"No," replied Mehul nonchalantly, "you will be ready when you will be able to do the same thing back home."

"It's impossible to please you, isn't it?" said Suraj with a chuckle.

THE LONG VIGIL

It was the last ball of the day. The bowler bowled a ball wide outside the off-stump. Suraj slashed hard at the ball intending to dispatch the ball to the fence. But instead of hitting the ball, his bat swung in the air not making contact. Mehul, who was batting at the other end, angrily waved his bat at Suraj and said loudly, "What the hell do you think you're doing?"

It was a lucky reprieve for Suraj who had an average of 9.56 with the bat in the five matches that Yorkshire had played. Yorkshire's score was 155 for five wickets at the end of the fourth day of play. They were at the bottom of the table and desperately needed a win. A large part of why they did not do well was Suraj's inability to contribute with the bat. Suraj had decided to play the enforcer in the series and had tried to score at a brisk pace. But instead of reaping dividends, the move led to him getting out cheaply every time and it certainly did not help the team as they would lose their remaining wickets in a matter of minutes.

"End of day's play," announced the umpire and removed the bails from the top of the stumps.

Suraj gingerly walked towards Mehul who was standing at the other end, breathing heavily in an attempt to control his temper. Mehul had told him earlier that he should refrain from playing any rash shots and Suraj had not listened to it. Luckily Mehul didn't say another word as they made their way towards the Dressing Room. After changing their clothes, Mehul and Suraj drove back to their building. They didn't say a single word to each other as they went into their respective apartments.

Half an hour later, Suraj heard a soft knock on his door. He looked through the peep hole and saw that it was Mehul. He opened the door and let his teammate inside his apartment. Mehul sat on the chair next to the bed and took a deep breath. Suraj held his breath, having a feeling that Mehul would explode with rage. But instead, Mehul spoke in a soft but firm voice.

"Do you have a death wish, Suraj?" asked Mehul.

"What?" asked Suraj surprised.

"Do you know what your batting average is this season?" he asked .

"I don't know," replied Suraj.

"It is 9.56," said Mehul calmly looking at Suraj straight in the eye. "You must do something about that."

"Okay," replied Suraj.

"When you go out to bat tomorrow, I don't want you to play a single shot on the off side," said Mehul.

"But-" protested Suraj.

"I'm not asking you. I'm telling you, Suraj," asserted Mehul, "you will not play a single shot on the off side and neither will you play a single attacking shot."

"Then how will I score?" asked Suraj.

"Graft, dammit," said Mehul, "graft like you did against the Kiwis at Kolkata. That was beautiful!"

"What if I get out?" asked Suraj.

"Aren't you already getting out?" asked Mehul sternly. "You are not an attacking batsman, Suraj, so don't act like one. Your strength is defence. You can't hit your way out of a rut; you must graft your way out of it."

"Okay," said Suraj reluctantly.

"Now tell me how you will play tomorrow," said Mehul.

"I will not play an attacking shot," said Suraj half heartedly.

"And?" said his teammate.

"I won't play on the off side," said Suraj.

"Okay," said Mehul. "You still want to play for India don't you?"

"Obviously!" said Suraj irritably. "What kind of a question is that?"

"Then you must do as I say," said Mehul.

"Okay," replied Suraj.

"Now, we need another 165 runs to win tomorrow," said Mehul.

"I know," said Suraj.

"Just hear me out Suraj," said Mehul, "just listen to me."

"Okay," said Suraj.

"It means that we must score at a run rate of 1.8 per over," said Mehul.

"So?" asked Suraj, not understanding what Mehul wanted to say.

"I'm saying that tomorrow we must play the waiting game," said Mehul, "we must play patiently tomorrow. No need to do anything fancy. Understood?"

"Yes," replied Suraj.

"Good," said Mehul and got up, "see you tomorrow. Good night."

"Good night Mehul," said Suraj and opened the door for his teammate.

The next morning, Mehul faced the first ball of the day and nudged the ball to third man for a single. As Suraj took strike, he looked around the field seeing as to where the fielders were placed. He noticed that there was no fielder at point. He decided that if he got a ball outside the off stump, he would slash hard and hope to dispatch the ball to the fence.

The bowler took his long run up and bowled the ball wide outside the off stump. Suraj's eyes lit up. It was exactly what he had hoped for. Ignoring the instructions which Mehul had given him the night before, he slashed hard, but instead of hitting the ball in the middle of the bat, the ball kissed the outside edge of the bat and went straight into the palms of the wicket keeper. The opposing Team erupted in glee. Mehul shouted loudly in frustration.

"No ball," said the umpire.

"What?" said the Captain of the opposing Team.

"No ball," repeated the umpire, his right arm outstretched.

"What the fuck!" shouted the Captain in frustration.

"Mind your language, young man," said the umpire to the Captain sternly.

"Sorry," said the Captain and walked back to his fielding position in the slips.

Mehul angrily walked to Suraj and in a soft voice, "the next time you try something like that, I swear I will shove this bat right up your ass."

"Sorry Mehul," said Suraj apologetically.

"Have you forgotten what I told you yesterday?" asked Mehul sternly.

"No," replied Suraj.

"Repeat what I said," instructed Mehul.

"I won't play a single attacking shot," said Suraj.

"And?" asked his teammate.

"I won't play a single shot on the off side," said Suraj.

"Good," said Mehul, "now get on with it."

The next hour was hell for Suraj. Every time he was on strike, the bowler would deliberately bowl wide outside the off stump in anticipation that Suraj would slash hard. But Suraj maintained a tight control on his instincts. While there was a deep desperation inside him for getting runs, the prospect of seeing Mehul angry again was enough motivation for him to play the waiting game. But it was very frustrating.

"What should I do?" asked Suraj in between overs, feeling helpless.

"Do as I said," replied Mehul calmly, "don't worry."

"Okay," replied Suraj half heartedly.

"Hey Suraj," said Mehul, "I've also gone through the same phase. I know it's not easy. But there's no other way. You must scrap it out."

"If you say so," said Suraj and walked towards the stumps and took guard.

It took some time, but the patience of the bowlers finally wore out. Their line and length started to waver and Suraj capitalized. Slowly but surely, his score increased. When it was lunch time, he score was 27 runs off 126 balls.

"Well done Suraj," said Mehul, patting Suraj's back as they walked off the field for the lunch break.

"Thanks," replied Suraj, relieved that he had survived the session.

"Now continue the same in the next session," said Mehul.

"Okay," replied Suraj.

During the lunch break, it started raining. Luckily it rained for only fifteen minutes, but that was enough for it to change the conditions of play completely. When they went back on to the field post lunch, Suraj felt a nip in the air. Sensing that the conditions had turned in their favour, the bowling side got their tails up and went for the kill.

"Goddammit!" shouted Suraj as another ball hit him in the ribcage, half an hour later. The bounce had become uneven with most of the balls staying low while the odd ball rose alarmingly.

"What happened?" asked Mehul as he rushed down the pitch, concerned.

"The pitch is behaving like a bitch!" said Suraj, hunched over.

"I know," said Mehul with a wry smile. "Hang in there buddy," he said patting Suraj on the back.

"That's it?" asked Suraj with a chuckle. "No motivating speech to help me out of this rut?"

"Motivation only lasts so long Suraj. You must grind it out," suggested Mehul. "Take it one ball at a time, one over at a time."

"Okay," said Suraj as he stood upright.

"Hey Suraj," said Mehul.

"Yeah?" said Suraj.

"You're doing great, hang in there," replied Mehul and walked back to the non-striker's end.

Suraj took guard once more and took a deep breath. He did not feel even a little confident. He had scored close to 40 runs by then, but the going had been horrendous. The next ball stayed low and hit him squarely on his box.

"Motherfucker!" shouted Suraj loudly in pain.

"Play the ball at the last moment," said Mehul an hour later at the next drinks break.

"You could have told me that a little earlier you know," said Suraj as he took a sip of an energy drink.

"Hey Suraj," said the player who had brought out the drinks.

"Yeah?" said Suraj and looked at him.

"Coach says that you are doing a great job," said the player. "He told you to hang in there."

"Okay, if you say so," said Suraj half-heartedly.

"Come on, time to get back to work," said Mehul after a while.

Suraj had now got himself stuck in a hole and didn't how to get out of it. He was stuck on the score of 49 for half an hour and had faced a total of 201 balls.

"Don't ask me what my strike rate is," said Suraj with a chuckle between the overs.

"Don't worry about that," said Mehul reassuringly. "That's not important."

"How long to tea?" asked Suraj.

"I think two more overs," replied Mehul.

"Hmm," said Suraj.

"Accept the struggle Suraj, embrace it. The more you fight it, the harder you will make it for yourself."

Those words of Mehul rung through Suraj's mind as he walked towards the wicket. Why was he kicking himself for struggling? The next ball he faced pitched halfway down the wicket and bounced towards his head. He swerved his head out of the way and heaved a huge sigh of relief. The ball after that bounced at a good length and swung into him. He shuffled across the stumps and worked the ball off his hips to fine leg. When he ran to the other end, he noticed that the people in the stands stood up and started applauding. Mehul also ran down the length of the wicket and congratulated Suraj.

"Why are they clapping? What happened?" asked Suraj.

"You've scored a half century," said Mehul, a huge smile on his face.

"Well played champ," said a player of the opposition and walked up to Suraj and patted him on the back. All the players of the opposition then walked up to him and congratulated him.

"Are they making fun of me?" asked Suraj after the players had disbursed.

"Are you kidding?" said Mehul. "That's the best innings I've seen in a long time!" he said enthusiastically.

"Okay," said Suraj half-heartedly.

"Raise your bat dammit," said Mehul, "acknowledge the crowds."

"Oh yes," said Suraj and raised his bat to the crowd. When he turned towards the pavilion, he noticed that all the players of his team were also standing and applauding him. That helped raise his spirits a little bit.

"We need four runs to win Suraj!" said Mehul excitedly to Suraj after a couple of hours.

"What? So fast?" asked Suraj, who had lost track of time.

After Suraj hit the winning runs, he heaved a huge sigh of relief. For the first time in his life he had batted for the entire day. When they were walking towards the Dressing Room he noticed that all the players from his Team had come out and were standing at the edge of the boundary ropes. When they reached the ropes, the opposition team stopped.

"After you champ," said the Captain of the opposing team to Suraj.

"Thanks," said Suraj and shook his hand.

"That was an awesome innings," he said, "it was inspirational."

Suraj then shook the hands of all the opposition players and was greeted enthusiastically by his teammates. When he reached the coach of the Team, he hugged Suraj even though he was dripping with sweat.

"Amazing job, my boy," said the coach," awesome!"

"Thanks Coach," replied Suraj, still in his own world.

After having a shower and changing his clothes, Suraj sat down in the pavilion and looked out at the ground. It was only then that he noticed that he was feeling mentally and physically exhausted. However, when he was playing he hardly noticed any physical fatigue. But now, every part of his body ached. He then felt a hand on his shoulder. It was Mehul.

"What just happened, Mehul?" asked Suraj, still in a trance. "What did I just do?"

"You went into something that we call *The Zone*," said Mehul.

"What is it?" asked Suraj.

"It is when all you care about is the next ball you are going to face," explained Mehul. "It is when your entire mind, body and soul focus on one thing and one thing only."

"Okay," said Suraj.

"So what do you think?" asked Mehul.

"I don't know what to think," replied Suraj, "I'm blank. My mind is empty."

"Good," said Mehul. "Do you know what you just did Suraj?"

"What?" asked Suraj and turned to his teammate.

"You were meditating," he replied.

BACK IN CONTENTION

Suraj picked up his cell phone and dialed Aditi's number.

"I got selected," said Suraj excitedly.

"Don't shit with me Suraj; it's not on the news," she shot back irritably.

"I know, it's not been shown on the news yet," he replied, "I got a call from the Selection Committee."

"So you're not screwing with me right?" asked Aditi, sounding a little excited.

"Not even a little bit," replied Suraj.

"That's great!" she said loudly, now barely able to mask the excitement in her voice.

"And all credit goes to you," said Suraj sincerely. "If you hadn't kicked some sense into me, I would have quit long ago."

"Oh shut up," she replied playfully.

"So, may I have the pleasure of meeting you?" asked Suraj.

"No," was her short reply.

"What?" replied Suraj.

"Take me out for dinner, you idiot," she replied laughing loudly.

"That's it?" he replied feeling slightly more relaxed.

"Obviously, what else?" she said.

"Okay, I think I can do that," he replied, "what time should I pick you up?"

"How about 8 pm?" asked Aditi.

"Sure," replied Suraj and hung up.

At about 8 pm that evening, Suraj parked his car outside Aditi's clinic in Opera House.

"Where are you?" he asked her on his cell phone.

"I'll be there," she replied, "I'm just climbing down the stairs."

Suraj got out of the car and stood, leaning against it. About a minute later, he saw her thin form walking through the gate.

"You did it!" she squealed and caught him in a tight embrace.

"No, we did it," replied Suraj.

"Come, let's go and celebrate!"

"Where do you want to go?" he asked as they sat in the car.

"I know just the place," she replied as she put on her seat belt.

Fifteen minutes later, they were sitting in a dimly lit pub.

"Are you sure about this place?" asked Suraj, not comfortable with the smell of alcohol in the air.

"Oh come on, relax!" replied Aditi cheerfully, "I've come here plenty of times, it's a great place to have a party."

"You've come here plenty of times?" asked Suraj, giving her with a questioning look, "You're not so innocent after all."

"Hey, I never claimed to be innocent," she replied immediately. "You just assumed that I was innocent."

The waiter then walked up to them to take their order.

"Would you like something to drink?" he asked.

"I'll have a Scotch on the rocks," said Aditi.

"Pepsi for me," said Suraj.

"Come on Suraj, we're celebrating today," said Aditi, "get him a beer," she said to the waiter.

"No, I'm not drinking," replied Suraj firmly.

"Come on, it's only one beer," she pressed on.

"No," he replied, this time even firmly. "Get me a Pepsi," he said to the waiter.

"Hey aren't you Suraj Bhatkal?" asked the waiter, recognising him.

"Yeah," replied Suraj.

"Could I have a photograph with you please?" was the waiter's next question.

"Sure," replied Suraj, "why don't you come here?" he said pointing to the seat next to him.

The waiter, clearly star struck handed his cell phone to Aditi, his hands shaking and said, "Could you please take a photograph?"

"Sure," she said and took the photograph.

As the waiter walked away, Suraj called him and said, "Could you not mention to anybody that I'm here? I want to spend a quiet evening."

"Sure Sir, no problem," replied with the waiter.

They spent the next few hours chatting away.

THE COMEBACK

Suraj sat in a corner of the dressing room of the Indian cricket team and looked around. He was there after a gap of nearly two years.

"Suraj, come here!" said Vikrant, the captain.

"Yeah," said Suraj walking across the room.

"You have been selected in the playing eleven," said Vikrant.

"Thanks," replied Suraj, his face not displaying the happiness he was feeling.

"I heard that you learnt reverse swing. Is it true?"

"Yeah, I did learn it," replied Suraj.

"Hmm," said Vikrant, in deep thought. "I also want you to be in charge of shining the ball."

"Sure," he replied.

"But that means that you will have to stand at mid-on or mid-off where you won't get a breather between overs," said Vikrant.

"That won't be a problem," replied Suraj.

"Great!" said the captain with a smile and walked away after patting Suraj on the shoulder.

West Indies won the toss and decided to bat first. The opening batsmen batted well, scoring 74 runs at a brisk pace when Suraj was given the chance to bowl. He measured 15 steps from the crease and placed a marker on the spot.

"Shortened your run up huh?" said Vikrant with a chuckle, who was standing next to Suraj to discuss the field setting.

"Yeah," replied Suraj with a grin.

"What field do you want?" asked Vikrant.

Suraj had been planning for this moment for the last two years. He set up the field in less than a minute as Vikrant gesticulated with his arms, moving fielders to the desired positions. Suraj closed his eyes and took a couple of deep breaths. He then looked at the ball and smiled as he had maintained it perfectly with one side shiny and the other side scuffed up. Suraj placed the ball in his left hand in such a way that the batsman couldn't see which side the shine was. He took one last look at the field, ensuring that all the fielders were standing at their instructed positions. He felt a tingle of excitement through his body as it was his chance to put into action everything he had learnt in Yorkshire.

Suraj ran at a brisk pace towards the crease and bowled a ball which landed at just outside off stump and swung into the right-handed batsman at the last moment. The batsman, looking at Suraj's short run up had estimated that the speed of the ball would not be fast. It is commonly but wrongly thought that the speed of the delivery is directly proportional to the length of the run up of the bowler. The reflexes of the batsman was half a second slower than required. The ball was bowled at a speed of 145 kmph and it was quick enough to bamboozle the batsman, who played a forward defensive shot in the hope of smothering the swing of the ball. But the high speed of the ball together with late swing resulted in the batsman not connecting bat to ball. Instead, the ball hurtled beyond the bat and crashed into the off stump causing it to be uprooted.

Suraj, the rest of the Indian team and the 60,000 odd spectators in the Eden Gardens stadium in Kolkata exulted in joy as the off stump cart wheeled towards the wicket keeper. He had taken a wicket off the very first delivery of his comeback match.

Suraj went on to take two more wickets in the same over off alternate balls. The first of them was nearly identical to the one which dismissed the opening batsman. But the third wicket was described by the commentators as one of the best they had seen in recent years. The ball pitched on middle stump and swung away late from the right-handed batsman to crack the off stump in half. The West Indies had lost three wickets in a space of five deliveries and it was Suraj who was the destroyer-in-chief.

The West Indies was bundled out for a paltry score of 148 and Suraj took 6 wickets in the innings. After the end of day's play, Suraj spoke to the rest of the team about his experiences in Yorkshire and explained to them the importance of county cricket in a player's development. Vikrant, who was listening attentively during the time that Suraj was speaking, said that he would like the other fast bowlers in the team to also go and play at least one season of County Cricket to sharpen their skills.

THE PROMOTION

For the next few months, Suraj performed with distinction with both bat and ball. However, India failed to win a single series in this time, and there were calls for the captain to be removed. Suraj was invited to the BCCI Headquarters by the President at this time.

Aditi drove Suraj to the BCCI Headquarters and parked the car. Suraj, who was sitting in the passenger seat, was in thought and shaking his legs due to restlessness. Despite being one of the most consistent performers in the Team with both bat and ball ever since his comeback, Suraj always harboured a fear of being dropped from the side. And such meetings with the President of the BCCI with no mentioned agenda made his mind go into overdrive causing him to speculate. Sensing his nervousness, Aditi leaned over and put a comforting hand on his shoulder. She was the only person with whom he could discuss his fears and worries and she provided him with advice which helped him to temporarily quell the demons in his mind.

"Hey, it'll be okay," she said reassuringly, "I'm sure he just wants to catch up with you."

"Catch up?" said Suraj with surprise, his legs still shaking. "Why would the President of the BCCI want to catch up with me?" he said burying his hand in his face, unable to deal with the tension.

"You have spoken to him before, haven't you?" she asked.

"Yes, I have," replied Suraj sounding worried, "but not like this. Not one on one."

"Listen to me," she said, her voice more firm than before, "look at me, Suraj!" she said with a hint of irritation in her voice.

"What?" he asked, turning towards Aditi.

"No matter what happens today, whether you are dropped from the team, which for your information I don't think will happen, or made the Captain of the team or whatever, I will always be there with you. It won't make a difference to me whether you are playing for India or not," she said looking into his eyes, "you are my friend and I will never ditch you."

"You really think they'll make me the Captain?" asked Suraj, his face breaking into a naughty grin.

"Oh really, that's all you took from what I said?" said Aditi in irritation. "God you are hopeless!"

"Oh come on!" he said playfully putting his arm around her shoulder.

"Okay," she replied, giving a small smile.

They spent the next couple of minutes in silence and looked out at the sea in front of them. Within no time, Suraj started shaking his legs again, prompting Aditi to put a hand on his leg to make him stop. The frown on his forehead had reappeared and inspite of the air conditioner being set at the coolest temperature, a single bead of sweat made its way down from the right side of his temple down his jaw.

"I guess I better get going," he said and removed his seatbelt, "don't want to get lectured on the importance of punctuality."

Half an hour later, Suraj was still sitting on a comfortable sofa in the reception area. He removed his cell phone from his pocket and called Aditi.

"Where are you?" he asked.

"Outside," she replied, "why?"

"I may take some time here," said Suraj.

"Yeah, no problem," replied Aditi, "I'll wait."

"But what about your patients?" he asked.

"Don't worry about that," she said, "Dad can handle one day without me."

"See, it's okay, you can leave," said Suraj, "there's no need to wait for me."

"Suraj, didn't I tell you that I'll wait," she replied, sounding adamant, "you take your time, don't worry about me."

"But you'll get bored," replied Suraj, feeling guilty at the prospect of making Aditi wait for him.

"Suraj, this is the last time I'll say it," said Aditi, her voice extremely firm, "I'm going to wait outside no matter how much time it takes. You don't worry about me."

"Okay," he replied.

After a few minutes, the receptionist turned to Suraj and said, "Mr. Bhatkal, he's called you in."

Suraj got up from the comfortable couch and started shaking his arms like a windmill. The receptionist looked at his actions with curiosity.

"Just trying to get the blood flow going," said Suraj looking embarrassed.

Suraj followed the receptionist, who was standing a few feet away. She opened the door behind her desk for Suraj to walk through.

"Ah, come on in Suraj," said the President of the BCCI, a legendary opening batsman famed for his defensive batting.

"Hello Sir," said Suraj, in awe of the man, thinking that he was smaller than he had thought.

"Nice to finally meet you," said the President as he gave Suraj a firm handshake and motioned him to take a seat.

"The pleasure's mine, Sir," replied Suraj as he sat down.

"What would you like to have?" asked the President, pressing a button on his table, "tea, coffee, a soft drink or if you like, something else."

"Coffee will do, Sir," replied Suraj, surprised with the man's friendly behaviour.

"Bring two coffees," said the President in Marathi to a peon who just entered the room.

"But make mine strong with extra sugar," added Suraj also in Marathi.

"I hope I'm not driving you to sleep," said the President with a chuckle.

"Oh no Sir," he replied, going red in the face.

They spent the next few moments in silence. Suraj looked around the room, trying hard to avoid the President's x-ray eyes which were observing him closely.

"When did you start playing cricket?" asked the man, finally breaking the silence.

"When I was in the eighth grade, Sir," replied Suraj nervously sitting on the edge of his chair.

"Which school were you in?"

"St. Mary's ICSE, Sir."

"Oh, that's a nice school," said the President, "right at the bottom of the bridge right?"

"Yes Sir," replied Suraj, feeling a little more at ease.

"Our schools had a big rivalry back in the day," he said with a warm smile. Suraj smiled back.

"So your father is a Doctor?" asked the President.

"Yes," replied Suraj.

"Do you stay together?" he asked.

"Uh, actually we stay apart," replied Suraj awkwardly, not willing to talk about his father.

"And what about your mother?" was the next question.

"She died when I was a baby," replied Suraj, getting uneasy with the line of questioning.

The next couple of minutes were again filled with silence. Suraj once again looked around the room, trying to avoid eye contact with the batting legend.

"Now let's get down to business," said the President finally, "you must be wondering why I called you here just to chit chat about your family history."

"Not at all, Sir," lied Suraj, relieved that they had finally gotten down to the reason. However, within a split second, his heart starting beating faster and he had a sick feeling in his stomach as he remembered his fears of being dropped from the team.

"What is your opinion about leadership?" asked the President.

"I'm sorry Sir?" asked Suraj taken aback by the question.

"What do think about leadership?" asked the President again patiently. "What makes a good leader?"

"I'm sorry, Sir, I've never really thought about that," was Suraj's feeble response.

"Why don't you give it a thought," suggested the man in charge of the richest cricketing body in the world.

"Uh, I think a leader should be like a friend to his team mates," said Suraj after thinking for a while.

"Okay," said the President nodding his head, "anything else?"

"I also believe that a leader should be part of the team and not be aloof from the rest of the team members," added Suraj.

"That's nice," said the President straightening up and placing his elbows on the table in front of him, "I like your line of thinking."

"Thank you, Sir," replied Suraj, again wondering when he would get to the point.

"You know Suraj, I've been very busy this morning," said the President pouring himself a glass of water, "I've met every player who has played even one match for the country in the last one and a half years."

"Okay Sir," said Suraj, his mind still at sea.

"And I have asked each one of them the same question, who is that person who can lead our team to glory in the coming years," he said.

"Yes but, isn't Vikrant the captain?" asked Suraj, wondering why the President would ask such a question to the members of the team when they already had a Captain for all three formats of the game.

"That's the point I'm trying to make Suraj," said the President, "Vikrant is being dropped from the team. He has not been able to deliver for the last couple of years."

"But there's nothing in the news!" said Suraj, shocked.

"That's what is called a media clampdown," replied the President with a chuckle.

"My God, I can't believe this," said Suraj, in shock.

"So coming back to my point," said the President, appearing calm as ever as he leaned back into his large cushioned chair which enveloped his small frame, "I asked the boys whom they would like as their next Captain."

"So what did they say?" asked Suraj.

"Before I tell you what they said, I want to ask you, Suraj," said the President, "who do you think is a good candidate for being the next Captain?"

Suraj thought for a while and said, "Don't know Sir."

"I asked the same question to every other member of the Team," said the President. "Do you want to know what they said?"

"Yes, please!" was the impatient reply from the young cricketer.

"You," said the President, straight faced.

"Me? What about me?" asked Suraj, confused.

"They want you to be the Captain," he said.

"Okay," replied Suraj, completely taken by surprise.

"Okay what?" said the President, "what do you think?"

"Think about what Sir?" asked Suraj, his mind still spinning.

"Do you accept the offer of being India's next Captain?"

"So, what did he want to talk to you about?" asked Aditi half an hour later as Suraj seated himself beside her in the car. But Suraj did not respond. Instead, he continued looking ahead, his eyes blank as he saw the Arabian Sea in front of them.

"Suraj," said Aditi, shaking Suraj by the shoulders, "what did he say?"

"Oh, uh, yeah," stammered Suraj, coming out of his trance.

"Tell me," pressed on his friend.

"He wants to make me Captain," said Suraj, a blank expression on his face.

"Yes! That's great!" said Aditi and hugged him.

"Yeah," said Suraj, "but I don't know if I'll accept it or not."

"Why not?" she asked. "It's an amazing opportunity."

"I've never captained any team and plus I've only been back a year now," said Suraj.

"Listen," said Aditi and took Suraj's hand into hers, "I think you'll do an awesome job."

"Isn't it obvious that you will say that? You're my friend!" said Suraj.

"Do you think I've always praised you Suraj?" she said. "Haven't I told you every time you have done something shitty and stupid? Don't you trust me even this much?"

"I trust you," said Suraj.

"Then what do you think?" said Aditi excitedly. "Will you take the job?"

"Yes," replied Suraj.

"That's awesome!" said Aditi and hugged him again.

Later that evening, Suraj sat on the comfortable arm chair in his house and was scrolling through the channels. Wondering what the press was going to say about him being made captain, he switched to the news channels.

"Suraj Bhatkal is at best overrated," said one panelist, a former cricketer. "His batting is boring and his bowling is not that great either."

"And he has never captained any team," said the second panelist, "not even his school team."

Suraj felt a sense of dejection as he heard the panelists criticise his lack of leadership experience. He then felt his cell phone vibrate. It was Aditi.

"Are you watching the news?" asked Suraj instantly.

"Don't watch the news, Suraj," replied Aditi. "They don't know what they are talking about."

"But they're right," said Suraj, "I've never captained any team and now they want me to captain India. I mean how can I do it?"

"I think you'll do a great job," said Aditi reassuringly.

"You're just saying that so that I feel better," said Suraj.

"No, I'm saying it because I know you Suraj," said his friend. "I think there is nobody better qualified than you."

"Why?" asked Suraj.

"It's because you have struggled in your life," said Aditi, "nothing has come easy to you. You will understand what a fellow player is thinking when he is going through a rough patch. Not many people understand people the way you do Suraj."

"Do you really think so?" asked Suraj, his spirits rising.

"Yes, I really do feel that," replied Aditi. "And I'm not saying this just so that you feel better. I am saying it because it's the truth."

"Okay, if you say so," said Suraj.

Suraj felt a wave of gratitude to the only true friend he had. Being a sportsman was lonely, and with the whole country either praising or abusing you, it was easy to get carried away. It was important to have an anchor, somebody one could hold on to in turbulent times when self-doubt could get the better of oneself. And for Suraj, that anchor was Aditi. Realising that the opinion of has-been cricketers was not consequential, Suraj changed the channel and watched a comedy movie.

THE RELUCTANT LEADER

Suraj's first assignment as India's Captain was the four match test series against Bangladesh, with the first Test being held in Eden Gardens, Kolkata. Suraj walked out onto the field on a hot and humid day in October 2025. The opposing Captain, the two umpires and cameramen accompanied him onto the field.

The match referee showed the two Captains the coin and tossed it up in the air.

"Heads," said Suraj.

"Heads it is," said the referee as the coin fell to the ground.

"What have you chosen to do?" asked the commentator to Suraj.

"We will bowl first," said Suraj.

A few minutes later, before the match commenced, the Indian players got into a huddle.

"So," said Suraj, looking at the players in the huddle. He wondered what he should say.

"Yes cap," said 17 year old Rizwan. Short and slightly chubby, Rizwan was the youngest and most enthusiastic member of the team. He was a child prodigy and had broken many records during his school days. He also scored centuries in each of the domestic tournaments like Ranji Trophy, Duleep Trophy, Irani Trophy and Syed Mushtaq Ali Trophy.

"Uh, as you know we have chosen to bowl," started Suraj softly. "Kevin and I will open the bowling. Is that okay with everyone?"

"Sure cap," said the rest of the Team.

"Okay, so let's do it," said Suraj and the huddle dispersed.

India won the 4 match Test series 1-0 without any significant opposition from Bangladesh. But the fact that Suraj was holding himself back as a leader had not escaped the attention of the coach, Mr. Singh. Mr. Singh spoke with the rest of team members and then he also had a conversation with Aditi. They agreed that Suraj had to become more assertive as a leader.

One morning when Suraj returned home, he saw that the coach and Aditi were waiting to meet him.

"Good morning Suraj," said Mr. Singh.

"Oh, hi," said Suraj, surprised to see the coach of the Indian Cricket team at his house.

"Please sit down Suraj," said Aditi, "we need to talk to you."

"Okay, but can I shower first?" asked Suraj.

"Yeah, sure," replied Aditi.

Suraj showered quickly and joined them.

"Okay, what do you want to talk about?" asked Suraj.

"It's about your captaincy," said Aditi.

"What about it?" asked Suraj, feeling his pulse quicken.

"I had a talk with the rest of the team and also with Aditi," said the Coach.

"We evaluated your performance as Captain in the Bangladesh series," said Aditi.

"What were your observations?" asked Suraj, taking a sip of water.

"We came to the conclusion that you must be more assertive," said Mr. Singh.

"Yes, and also stop asking for the team's approval before taking every decision," added Aditi.

"But shouldn't they be okay with my decisions? What if they don't like what I tell them?" asked Suraj.

"Suraj, you are the captain of the Indian cricket team," he said. "The boys will do anything you tell them. They respect you."

"Okay," replied Suraj.

"You must stop being so reluctant on the field. You are the leader of the team," he said. "Don't worry about what the others will think. You don't need anyone's approval for the decisions that you take."

"Really?" asked Suraj.

"Yes," replied the two of them.

"From now on I want to see you be more interactive and adventurous with your captaincy," said Mr. Singh. "I know that you can do it. You have good leadership skills."

"But my father said that I will never be a good leader," said Suraj.

"Suraj, listen to me," said Aditi and took his hand into hers. "To hell with what your father said."

"Okay," replied Suraj with a weak smile.

"Do you trust me?" asked Aditi.

"Yes," he replied.

"Then will you do as we say?" she asked.

"Yes," replied Suraj.

"Good," said the Coach.

From then on, it was like a weight was lifted off Suraj's shoulders. He became adventurous in his captaincy and started taking more risks. He adopted the strategy of winning at all costs. That was what India needed desperately in the grueling Tours to come.

THE LOST OPPORTUNITY

India's Tour of South Africa in December 2025 was a series which all cricket lovers were looking forward to. Suraj travelled to South Africa with a few test specialists from the team in advance to get acclimatised to the conditions there. He pushed his team to work overtime to get acquainted with the bouncy nature of the South African tracks.

The Test Series was a see-saw affair, with neither team being able to gain the upper hand for a sustained period of time. As a result, the first two tests end up in a draw. But in the third test, India gained the upper hand for most of the match. On the last day, South Africa required around 300 runs to win with only 4 wickets in hand. Everyone expected India to win comfortably in the first session of the fifth day itself.

However, South Africa managed to scrape through the last day without losing a wicket. Even though South Africa didn't win the match, Suraj viewed it as a loss. Dejected, he wondered if he would ever lead India to a Test Series win outside the subcontinent.

THE GREAT ESCAPE

The next major series for India was the 4 test match tour of England in June 2026. To get acclimatised to the cold conditions which he thought he would encounter in England and to practice batting on spongy, green wickets in conditions favourable for swing bowling, Suraj went to Dharamshala for a month.

The first test at Southampton, ended up a draw as both sides played dull cricket. The second test at Edgbaston, was more competitive. England set India a target of 325 runs to win with 4 sessions of play remaining. As the Indian team sat in the Dressing Room, Suraj was calculating the required run rate in his mind.

T*here are roughly 120 overs to be played,* he thought to himself. *That means a run rate of about 2.8 runs per over. It's definitely doable.*

He stood up and cleared his throat. The rest of the Team stopped what they were doing and looked towards him.

"Guys, we have to score 325 runs in about 120 overs," said Suraj and started pacing around the room. "I didn't come here just to compete. I came here to win! So let's go out there and win this match!"

While the small speech had everybody pumped up, within moments, it started raining heavily. Suraj became worried and cursed the English weather as he recalled that it was warm and sunny just fifteen minutes earlier.

An hour later after the rain had subsided, the opening batsmen walked out to the pitch. Suraj's small speech had filled them with optimism. They were geared up and were ready to face any situation, including the moist air and spongy wicket. But, as the cliché goes, *cricket is a funny game.* Fortunes change in an instant in this game that depended largely on atmospheric and weather conditions.

Two wickets fell in quick succession. Suraj was worried. The change in weather conditions had dampened his plans. He had hoped that the opening batsmen would set up a good foundation of runs for the middle order to build on. But it wasn't to be. He had a conversation with the two opening batsmen once they got back and changed their clothes.

"Sorry, Cap," said one of the opening batsmen, feeling disappointed.

"It's okay," replied Suraj who looked back and smiled, "you did your best."

"What should I do, Cap?" asked Rizwan, the next batsman.

"Go for the win Riz," replied Suraj and patted him on the back.

"You got it boss," replied Rizwan and walked out onto the field.

A moment later, as Suraj was drinking water, Mr. Singh, the Coach called him urgently.

"Suraj! A wicket has fallen!" said the Coach.

"Okay," said Suraj, had a quick sip of water, put on his helmet and checked his gear.

"What's the plan Suraj?" asked the Coach as Suraj put on his gloves.

"We're going for the win," replied Suraj and walked out.

"How's the pitch?" asked Suraj to Rizwan as he walked onto the pitch.

"Can't make out, Cap," replied Rizwan, "it's uneven. One ball stays low and the other ball bounces too much."

"Hmm," replied Suraj and evened out the pitch with his bat, "what about the swing?"

"It's swinging too much," he replied.

"Hmm," said Suraj, in deep thought. "Watch the ball till the last moment and then play it."

"Yes, Cap," replied Rizwan and started walking back to the other end when he stopped, turned around and asked Suraj, "Uh, Cap, what's the plan?"

"What do you mean?" asked Suraj.

"Are we going for the win?" he asked.

"Yes," replied Suraj.

"Okay, Cap," replied Rizwan and walked back to the other end of the pitch.

But the going was not at all easy for either of them as the ball swung around viciously at extreme pace. The rain had caused the temperature to drop and the moisture in the air to rise. The conditions were now perfect for swing bowling and made batting hell. Suraj had to use all of his experience to navigate the hostile English bowling. But even after using every ounce of his concentration and application, he managed to score only 15 runs in 83 deliveries. When the umpires announced the end of the day's play due to bad light, Suraj was a relieved man. India's score was 57 runs for the loss of 3 wickets after having played out 31 overs.

"What's the matter Suraj?" asked Mr. Singh later, looking at the worried look on Suraj's face.

"We can't win this match, boss," said Suraj, a frown etched on his forehead.

"Why not?" he asked.

"It's not possible," said Suraj, "the conditions are too hostile."

"What do you have in mind?" asked the Coach.

"We have to play for a draw," said Suraj, "I can't think of any other way out."

"Do whatever you think is right Suraj," he said. "You have my full support. Do you want me to tell the Team?"

"No, it's okay," replied Suraj and got up, "I'll inform them."

After informing the Team that they had to change their strategy from winning to saving the match, Suraj went to his room. The weather had changed once more. It was raining heavily now and there was a nip in the air as the temperature dropped. Suraj tossed and turned in his bed for a couple of hours. Then realising that sleep would not come to him, he got up and walked into the corridor of the hotel. Seeing that the light in Rizwan's room was on, he went ahead and knocked on the door.

"Who is it?" came a voice from the inside.

"It's me, Suraj," replied Suraj.

"Oh, come in Cap," said Rizwan as he opened the door and invited Suraj into his room.

Suraj stepped into Rizwan's room and saw that there were clothes and cricket gear scattered all round the room.

"Sorry for the mess," said Rizwan apologetically as he started removing the clothes off his bed and made space for Suraj to sit.

"It's okay," replied Suraj.

"What's up, Cap?" asked Rizwan. "Is there a problem?"

"There's no problem, Riz," replied Suraj, "I just couldn't sleep."

"Oh, you worried, Cap?" he asked.

"A little," said Suraj with a small smile.

"So uh, what do you want to do?" asked Rizwan.

"What do you do when you can't sleep?" asked Suraj.

"I play video games," said his teammate.

"Oh, which ones do you play?"

"GTA," replied Rizwan.

"GTA?" Suraj was clearly unfamiliar with that game.

"Yeah, Grand Theft Auto," said Rizwan.

Rizwan then took out his gaming console and connected it to the television.

"How do you play it?" asked Suraj and stood next to Rizwan.

"Here, I'll show you," said Rizwan and started explaining the controls of the joystick.

"Seems complicated," said Suraj, overwhelmed by the instructions.

"Oh it's easy," said Rizwan with a wave of his hand, "you'll get a hang of it."

"Okay, if you say so," said Suraj.

"Uh, you don't mind if we sit on the floor do you?" asked Rizwan awkwardly.

"Oh no," replied Suraj and sat on the floor. "So can we start?"

"Yeah," replied Rizwan and started a game.

They played until 2 am, when they realised that it was too late.

"Damn, I got to sleep now," said Suraj and put his joystick down.

"Yes, it's late," said Rizwan and switched off the gaming console.

"Good night Riz," said Suraj and got up.

"I hope you had a good time, Cap," said Rizwan.

"Oh yeah I did," said Suraj and smiled.

"Uh what should we do tomorrow?" asked Rizwan as Suraj was about to leave.

"What's the matter? Are you scared?" asked Suraj.

"Yeah, a little bit" he replied honestly.

"Don't worry, even I'm scared," said Suraj with a grin.

"Oh, I didn't know you also get scared," said Rizwan.

"The fear never goes, Riz," said Suraj. "Do you know what bravery is?"

"I guess it's the absence of fear," replied Rizwan.

"No, it's the ability to conquer your fear," explained Suraj. "Everybody gets scared. But you will rise above the others if you do not let your fear conquer you."

"I feel better now," said Rizwan, "I'm glad that I'm not the only person who is scared."

"Good night Rizwan," said Suraj and walked towards the door.

"Good night Cap," replied Rizwan and waved.

That night when Rizwan lay down on his bed; his fear was replaced by a sense of calm. That was his first overseas Tour. He felt a surge of gratitude towards his Captain because ever since he had made his debut in the Team at the age of 17, Suraj had always been present to solve doubts or problems. Suraj always answered his queries without hesitation and did not get irritated or angry when Rizwan asked many questions. As Rizwan closed his eyes, he was sure that he could do anything for his Captain. Anything.

The next day the English bowlers tried their best to win the match. But Suraj and Rizwan got stuck into the task of stonewalling them and soon the Englishmen got frustrated. When their attempts of getting out the two Indian batsmen failed, they resorted to abusing them. Suraj was used to this tactic and did not pay any attention to what the Englishmen said but Rizwan got extremely worked up.

After one over, the English bowlers got particularly nasty with their abuses and passed lewd comments about Rizwan's family members. This got him even more riled up. He walked over to them waving his bat at them and started shouting at his opponents, causing the umpires to intervene. They attempted to stand between the two opposing parties to stop them from fighting. However, it was only when Suraj got involved that Rizwan regained his composure.

"Calm down, Rizwan," said Suraj and firmly pulled his teammate away from the Englishmen.

"Didn't you hear what they said about my sister?" asked Rizwan, still fuming.

"That's their plan, Riz. They want you to get riled up so that you lose your focus," explained Suraj.

"Okay," said Rizwan, "what should I do?"

"Just focus on the next ball you are going to face, and don't react to what they say. The more you react, the more they will sledge you," said Suraj.

"Okay, Cap," replied Rizwan.

Suraj and Rizwan batted well into the last session of the day with both of them notching up half centuries. Rizwan managed to retain his composure and did not lose his cool even though the English bowlers and fielders continued to abuse him. When approximately twenty overs were left in the day, India suffered a mini collapse. They lost five wickets in the space of two overs. But Suraj was still around and that gave hope to the Indian supporters.

"How many overs are left?" asked Suraj .

"About twenty," replied the umpire.

"Thanks," said Suraj and walked over to Mahesh Srivastava, the batsman on the other end. Tall and lanky, Mahesh was another young member of the team and this was his first overseas tour. Even though he had a couple of half centuries in first class cricket at the domestic level, the international arena is a different ball game altogether.

"Listen Mahesh," said Suraj and looked at his fast bowling partner, "we have to play out the next twenty overs."

"Okay, Cap," replied Mahesh.

"If the ball is outside the off stump, leave the ball," instructed Suraj.

"Okay," he replied.

"And if the ball is bowled at the stumps, you block," said Suraj.

"Okay," replied the youngster.

"I hope you understand what I am saying," said Suraj, "don't try anything adventurous. Play safe. I don't care if you don't score any runs. The point now is not to score runs; it is to save the match and play out the remaining overs."

"Okay, Cap," said Mahesh, his voice shaking with fear.

"Hey don't worry," said Suraj reassuringly, "I'm not going anywhere. We can have a chat after every ball if it makes you feel better."

"Yeah, I'd like that," replied Mahesh with a weak smile.

After another tense 10 overs, the score was the same, as neither Suraj nor Mahesh scored any runs. But despite the lack of runs being scored; the spectators were glued to their seats. Suraj got a warning from the umpires for wasting time. This was because he talked to Mahesh after every ball, giving him instructions on how to face the next delivery. But the warnings didn't deter Suraj. He had only one thing on his mind, and that was to avoid defeat.

When about five overs were left, Mahesh got out, unable to keep out an inswinging yorker.

"Sorry, Cap," said Mahesh, dejected before he started walking to the pavilion.

"Don't worry Mahesh," replied Suraj reassuringly, "you played wonderfully. And listen, walk back slowly, we must use up as much time as we can."

"Okay, Cap," replied Mahesh and walked back slowly towards the pavilion.

Out walked Kevin, a large cricketer in front of whom the bat looked small. Suraj gave him the same instructions he had given Mahesh.

"No wild shots okay, no matter how loose they bowl," instructed Suraj, "your job is to keep the ball from touching the stumps. I don't care how you do it. I don't care if it's ugly."

"Sure, Cap," replied Kevin coolly.

Kevin was able to negotiate that over without incident, much to the delight of the Indian spectators. When Suraj prepared to face the next ball, his score was 79 runs of 452 balls. He had a strike rate of 17.48 per 100 balls, an innings slow even by Suraj's standards.

The bowler, the English Captain, took his long run up and delivered a ball pitching on middle stump and moving away from Suraj. Suraj played a backward defensive shot, but unfortunately the ball nicked the edge of the bat. Suraj's head snapped back; a reflex action which a batsman usually makes when he edges the ball. The ball went into the hands of the wicket keeper, who threw the ball up in the air in delight. The entire English Team ran towards the keeper to celebrate the catch. But the umpire was unmoved. He hadn't heard the edge. Suraj also stood his ground. If he would have taken even one step towards the pavilion, it would have meant that he acknowledged that he had edged the ball. The match would have been over and England would win. But Suraj stood where he was and looked around calmly.

"How's that umpire?" asked the bowler.

"Not out," said the umpire.

"What? But he nicked it!" said the bowler, not able to digest the verdict of the umpire.

"I said, not out," said the umpire once more.

The bowler walked up to Suraj menacingly and asked him, "you nicked it, didn't you?"

"Fuck you, Barbie doll," replied Suraj with a chuckle, still standing his ground.

"Fucking cheat," said the bowler and walked back shaking his head.

Kevin walked over to Suraj and asked him, "did you nick it?"

"Of course I nicked it," replied Suraj calmly, "everybody in the stands also knows it."

"Haha!" laughed Kevin, punched his fist with his Captain's and walked back to the other side of the pitch.

The two of them cautiously played out the remaining overs, talking after every ball, in the hope of using up as much time as they could. After about half an hour, the umpires removed a device from their pocket and looked at the reading. After consulting each other, the umpires decided that it was the end of the day's play.

"But the light is still good!" pleaded the Englishmen.

"Our decision is final; this is the end of day's play gentlemen," said the umpires firmly and removed the bails from the top of the stumps.

"Phew, we did it!" said Suraj and raised his hands in the air. Kevin ran over to Suraj and lifted him up in the air in celebration. Suraj had batted out the full quota 90 odd overs of that day to deny England a win.

When Suraj entered the dressing room, the team applauded him. His team mates kept saying that he was the reason why they drew the match. After he removed his gear, Suraj stood in the middle of the room and cleared his throat to speak. The rest of the Indian contingent, including the coaches, physios and managers were eager to listen to what their Captain had to say.

"I couldn't have done it without you guys today," said Suraj.

"Oh come on, Cap, now you're just being modest," said Rizwan with a chuckle.

"No, I'm not," said Suraj firmly. "We will do everything as a Team. If we win, we win as a Team. If we lose we lose as a Team. Everybody gets equal credit and blame for what happens. So I don't want to hear it that *I* drew the game today, because it's wrong. I couldn't have done it without Rizwan, Mahesh, Kevin and everyone else. Just like each and every body part has a role to play in making our bodies function, each of you also has a function in this team. Know what your role is, excel in that role and if you see anyone doing something incorrectly, tell them. If you are a bowler, work on your bowling, but don't ignore your batting. If you are a batsman, give tips to the bowlers to bowl better."

"So what should we do now, Cap?" asked Kevin quietly.

"Now? We party!" said Suraj and smiled.

THE FINAL TEST

The English and Indian cricket teams travelled to Old Trafford after the Third Test had ended in an uneventful Draw. The final test at Lords was a hot-tempered one with tempers flaring on both sides and insults being spewed with irreverence. The English captain, frustrated with his side's inability to run through India's batting line up, at a press conference called India a land of snake charmers. Suraj took huge offence to this statement and at another press conference said that England did not invent the game of cricket. Suraj claimed that cricket was in fact invented by the Indians. This infuriated the English to no end. Cricket was a game of prestige for them. To be told that it was not their invention after all was a huge slap on their face, and this irritated them to no end. Play had to be stopped for a few minutes on day three of this test when the spectators in the crowd started throwing empty beer bottles at the Indian fielders.

On the final day of the Test, the match was evenly balanced. England needed 225 runs with 7 wickets in hand. Suraj used all his experience to place attacking fields and commanded his bowlers to bowl wicket-taking deliveries. Even though wickets fell at regular intervals, the English scored runs at a steady pace.

In the last fifteen minutes of play, England needed 15 runs to win off 18 balls while India needed only 1 wicket to win. Both sides were at the mercy of the umpires, after having used up their DRS Reviews.

Suraj threw the ball to Kevin and instructed him to get the final wicket. Kevin bowled the over of his life, but was unable to get the wicket. At the end of the over, he walked to Suraj; his shoulders slumped and said that he was sorry that he couldn't achieve what his Captain had wanted him to. Suraj put his arm around the youngster's shoulder and told him not to worry and that he will get the chance to bowl the final over of the match to make amends.

Suraj himself bowled the second last over, but was unable to break the deadlock. He then handed the ball to Kevin, put his arm around his shoulder and told him once again to take the final wicket. 5 runs were required by England to win the match in the last over. 3 runs were taken off the first 5 balls, leaving them to get 2 runs to win off the last ball. Suraj and Kevin had a long conversation about field placements before the final ball was to be bowled. They were warned by the umpires about wasting more time but Suraj paid no heed to the warnings.

After making the final adjustments, Kevin took his long run up and bowled a delivery which landed on off stump and swung into the pads of the right handed batsman. The ball hit the pads of the batsman and the entire Indian Team appealed for an LBW, but the umpire was unmoved. Suraj shouted in frustration as the English batsmen successfully took 2 runs and started to celebrate, having won the hard fought tournament.

The Indian players were dejected and the Indian contingent of the crowd was silenced. Replays showed that the ball would have gone on and hit the middle stump. This infuriated Suraj even more. He felt a sense of anger, despair and helplessness.

In the dressing room, in the privacy of the toilet, Suraj started crying. It seemed to him that all the effort of the past five months had borne no fruit. After five minutes, when he came out, his eyes red, he observed that the rest of the players were also inconsolable.

Mr. Singh, the Coach walked up to Suraj and told him, "There is no need to attend the post-match ceremony if you don't want to."

"No," replied Suraj, "I will do it, don't worry."

"Okay," he replied.

When Suraj walked out onto the field, the English players started abusing him. Without thinking, Suraj raised his middle finger at them and walked away.

Unfortunately, this was the image of Suraj which the English media decided to run with the next day. At the post match presentation ceremony, Suraj kept his answers short, dignified and concise even though he was seething with uncontrollable anger.

DISAPPOINTMENT

Suraj sat in the first class lounge of London's Heathrow Airport waiting for his flight that was to take off to India. While the exclusivity of the lounge shielded Suraj from the attention of people in the airport who would have liked to have a glimpse of him, Suraj's morale was in shambles. He had spent the previous five months straining every muscle of his body and using up the reserves of his mental strength towards achieving his goal of winning a test series outside the Indian Subcontinent.

Even though Suraj's Captaincy and individual performance was lauded by one and all, it was not enough consolation as he felt the web of depression and disappointment engulf his mind. He picked up his cell phone and called the first name in the address book.

"Hello! Oh my God I've been trying to reach you since ages!" said Aditi in relief on the other end of the line.

Suraj felt a momentary surge of electricity run through his body as he heard her voice. He had missed her immensely.

"I've missed you so much!" said Aditi. Her voice was cracking with emotion.

Suraj remembered the sacrifices he had made in the months leading upto the Tour and felt a sense of despair as he realised that he had not achieved what he had set out to. Slowly, tears started to roll down his cheeks as he began sobbing uncontrollably.

"Suraj, what's the matter?" asked Aditi sounding concerned.

"I failed!" said Suraj, in between sobs.

"No Suraj you have not failed," she said hoping that it would make him feel better.

"I thought that if you worked hard you get what you want," sobbed the captain of the Indian cricket team.

"Such things happen sometimes, Suraj, don't worry, you'll succeed the next time," said Aditi, as she herself tried to control her emotions.

"I don't know if there will be another chance like this, Aditi," replied Suraj.

"There is always another chance, Suraj," replied his only friend.

"I don't know if I can do this again," said Suraj.

"Why don't you come home and we can talk about that, huh?" suggested Aditi.

There was silence on the other end of the line for a while. Suraj tried to get control over his emotions.

"Suraj, are you there?" she asked after a while.

"Yes I'm here," replied Suraj.

"Just come home and then we can discuss what to do in the future. Is that okay?" said Aditi, hoping that Suraj wouldn't take any impulsive decisions.

"Okay," he replied.

After talking for some more time, Aditi hung up. Aditi had been watching the news and media uproar over India being cheated off a win. After the call, she walked into the toilet where she buried her face in her hands and started crying inconsolably. She had watched Suraj's struggles and the way he fought his way back into the Indian Cricket team after a year of hardwork and toil. She had also seen the effort he had put in to maintain his form and fitness over a sustained period of time. To see him denied of the goal he was striving for made her sad and angry. As the tears streamed down her face, she wished she was in London next to Suraj, able to share his sorrow.

Suraj was the only passenger in the first class section of the British Airways A380. As the airplane was taxiing, he picked up a newspaper and in it saw the picture of England's captain holding the Pataudi Trophy with a triumphant smile. That image filled Suraj with a sense of rage and he wished there was something which could quell the fire of his emotions. After the flight had taken off, the airhostess walked upto Suraj with a trolley of beverages.

"Would you like something to drink, Sir?" she asked politely, with a thick London accent.

"Yes, give me vodka," replied Suraj.

"Here you go, Sir," she said as she poured the transparent liquid into a glass.

Suraj felt a burning sensation in his chest as he gulped down the transparent liquid in one go. After a while, he started to feel pleasantly light headed. He then pressed a button on his seat which beckoned the airhostess.

"Would you like something Sir?" she asked politely.

"Yes, give me some more," said Suraj pointing to the bottle of vodka.

As she poured the transparent spirit into the glass, he pointed to his glass and said, "Fill it up when it becomes empty." Suraj had finally found refuge in something that he could drown his sorrows in.

A few hours later in Mumbai, Aditi was waiting at the airport to receive Suraj. It had already been two hours so she walked up to the enquiry counter to check whether Suraj's flight had landed.

"The flight landed an hour ago ma'am," was the reply.

"Have all passengers left?" she asked.

"Yes, they should have left by now," was the reply.

Aditi walked back to the place where she was standing as she wondered where Suraj must be. She dialed his cell phone number once again but there was no response. Feeling frustrated, she walked back to her car and thought that Suraj must have already left from some other exit. She wondered if her friend was alright.

Sanjeev heard a knock on his door. He looked at his watch and saw that it was way past midnight. As he walked to the door, he wondered who it could be.

"Hi dad!" said Suraj, standing in the doorway.

"What are you doing here?" asked his father, surprised. "Shouldn't you be in England?"

"I just wanted to meet you," replied his son. "Is there something wrong with that?"

"No, come in," said Sanjeev.

When Suraj sat down, he reached into his bag and took out two bottles.

"What are those bottles for, Suraj?" asked Sanjeev apprehensively as he saw the two large bottles.

"To celebrate," replied Suraj and took a large swig from one of the bottles.

"Celebrate what?" asked his father.

"Oh come on dad, don't act stupid," said Suraj as he leaned back into the chair, "we lost the series remember?"

"So how is that something we celebrate?" asked Sanjeev.

"I failed. Isn't that something we should celebrate?" said an intoxicated Suraj.

"Suraj, are you drunk?" asked his father, his voice laced with concern.

"Don't ask such complicated questions, dad," replied Suraj.

"What's so complicated about that question?"

"See, my body mind complex may be under the influence of alcohol, but that doesn't mean that *I* am drunk," said Suraj.

"Suraj please stop talking nonsense," said his father forcefully.

"Oh yeah? Then how come it made sense when you used to say the same Goddamned thing huh?" said Suraj.

"Just calm down Suraj," said his father and walked towards him, "and give me that bottle."

"Don't you dare touch this bottle!" shouted Suraj.

Sanjeev took a step back and said, "Suraj, just calm down. Everything will be all right."

"I'm going to the toilet," said Suraj and got up.

"Okay," replied Sanjeev, who was at the receiving end of a drunken rant.

When Suraj went into the toilet and closed the door behind him, Sanjeev acted fast. He locked the door of the toilet from the outside and then dialed Aditi's number from his phone.

"Hello," said Aditi, wondering who could be calling her so late at night.

"Hello, I'm Sanjeev speaking," he said.

"I'm sorry, who?" she asked, confused.

"Suraj's father," he said.

"What happened uncle?" she asked.

"Please come here fast," he said.

"Why? What happened?" asked Aditi.

"Suraj is here," he said.

"What?" she said in surprise, "What is he doing there?"

"I don't know dear, but you have to come here fast," said Sanjeev frantically.

"Can you tell me what happened?" asked Aditi.

"He's here and he is very drunk," said Sanjeev as he explained everything that happened.

"Okay, I'll come there right away," said Aditi, "give me the address."

Aditi immediately left home with the intention of reaching Sanjeev's house at the earliest.

"Oh, thank God you are here," said Sanjeev, visibly relieved when he saw Aditi at the door barely fifteen minutes later.

"Where is he?" asked a concerned Aditi.

"He's in the toilet," explained Sanjeev, "I locked him there."

"What?" said Aditi, shocked.

"Well he was acting strange; I think he is drunk," he said.

"Open the door, I'll take it from here," said Aditi.

"What the hell was all that about?" asked Suraj loudly as he unsteadily walked out the toilet.

"Suraj dear, sit down," said Aditi.

"What are you doing here?" he asked her.

"Your father called me," she said.

"Why?" he asked.

"You are drunk, Suraj. Please sit down," as she steadied him down to a sofa.

"Hey I'm not drunk, my body mind complex is drunk," said Suraj.

"Suraj shut up!" said Aditi forcefully. "You will not talk such shit with me!"

"Okay," said Suraj, mellowing down.

"Now come with me," she said and held his hand.

"Where are we going?" he asked.

"We are going home," she said.

As they walked towards the door, Sanjeev called Aditi aside and profusely thanked her.

"No problem uncle," she replied and walked away.

When they entered Suraj's apartment, Suraj sat down on a chair and covered his face with his hands.

"What's the matter Suraj?" asked Aditi with concern as she knelt down beside him.

"I'm so tired," he said, his voice cracking.

"Then go to sleep," she said.

"I can't as my mind just keeps on racing," he said.

"Come on, I'll help you sleep," said Aditi and gently walked Suraj towards the bed.

When they reached his bed, Suraj lay down with his head on Aditi's lap.

"Aditi," said Suraj.

"Yes?" she said as she ran her hand through his hair.

"I missed you so much," he said.

"I missed you too dear," she said.

"Promise me something?" he said.

"What Suraj?" she said.

"Promise that you won't leave me," said Suraj.

"Why will I leave you?" asked Aditi.

"I mean, what if I quit playing tomorrow, will you leave me?" he asked.

"Listen Suraj," said Aditi and made him sit up. "No matter what you do, whether you play cricket or not, whether you do anything with your life or not, I will never leave you. I promise."

"Really?" he asked, tears streaming down his face.

"Yes, I'll never leave you," she said.

"Thanks!" he said as he hugged her.

"You are welcome," said Aditi hugging him back. "Come on, now go to sleep."

The next morning after Suraj woke up, he walked into the living room.

"Hey," said Aditi who was sitting on a comfortable chair while watching a movie.

"Hey," replied Suraj as he sat down next to her.

"How are you feeling?" she asked.

"A little nauseous," he said.

"So what's your plan for today?" asked Aditi.

"Don't know," replied Suraj and he started scrolling through the messages on his phone.

"Then let's go to my home and have breakfast," said Aditi.

"Hmm," replied Suraj still immersed in his cell phone.

"Listen to me dammit," said Aditi irritably and took the phone away from his hand.

"Okay, let us go," said Suraj and got up.

A few minutes later, they were outside the door of Aditi's apartment.

"Hello Suraj!" said Aditi's father cheerfully when he opened the door.

"Hello Doctor," said Suraj and walked in.

"Please have a seat," he said and motioned towards the sofa.

"Papa, what's there for breakfast?" asked Aditi and sat down next to Suraj.

"The same as every day, cornflakes and milk," replied her father.

"Can you make something for Suraj?" she asked, "something heavy. To uh, you know, get over a hangover."

"Oh surely," said her father. "Suraj, I'll make the best eggs you have ever had."

After a hearty breakfast, Suraj, Aditi and her father sat chatting around the table.

"Suraj, I want to tell you something," said Aditi's father.

"Sure Doctor," said Suraj, giving him his undivided attention.

"I'm really sorry for what happened in England," he said sincerely, "we all are."

"Thank you Doctor," replied Suraj.

"I don't remember the last time the public got so involved in cricket," he said.

"Hmm," said Suraj.

"But that being said, I don't think that is a good enough excuse for you to get drunk like you did," said Aditi's father.

"Yes Doctor, that was the first and last time," said Suraj, "it won't happen again."

"Good!" he said cheerfully.

Just then Suraj got a call. The call left him worried.

"What happened?" asked Aditi with concern.

"That was the BCCI," replied Suraj, his brow furrowed. "The President wants to see me."

"What does he want?" she asked.

"I honestly have no idea," he replied.

"Don't worry, I'm sure it's nothing serious," said Aditi reassuringly.

"Yeah," said Suraj still looking worried.

"When do you have to go?" she asked.

"I have to be there at 3 pm this afternoon," he replied.

"Great, so that gives us some time for you to get a shower and freshen up," she said.

"Yeah, I guess I should do that," replied Suraj and got up.

REASSURANCES

Aditi parked the car outside the rear entrance of the building. Suraj wanted to avoid the Press who were waiting at the front entrance. Suraj looked at the time. There was still half an hour left for the meeting with the President of the BCCI to start. He closed his eyes, rested his head on the headrest and took in deep breaths.

"Don't worry so much Suraj," said Aditi and placed her hand on his thigh.

"Yeah," said Suraj and opened his eyes.

They sat there for a while in silence.

"I guess I better go," said Suraj and opened the door.

"I'll wait for you," said Aditi.

"Oh no problem, you can go home, I'll get a cab or something on the way back," replied Suraj. "And anyways, don't you have your clinic?"

"I don't mind," replied Aditi, "I'll wait for you here."

"Okay," he replied and closed the door behind him.

A few moments later, Suraj was sitting in the reception area feeling tense, his legs shaking incessantly. He read on his cell phone that the ICC had started disciplinary proceedings against him, which made him even more worried.

"Mr. Bhatkal," said the receptionist, "the President has called you."

Suraj got up and opened the door.

"Come in, Suraj," said the President warmly and extended his right hand.

"Hello Sir," said Suraj and shook his hand.

"Please have a seat," said the President.

After indulging in small talk for a few minutes, the President of the BCCI cleared his throat and said, "Suraj, you must wonder why I called you here."

"Yes, Sir," replied Suraj, his throat dry.

"I followed the series very closely," said the President. "It was a hard fought series and you and the team played very well."

"Thank you Sir," said Suraj.

"But unfortunately we could not win," he said.

"Yes," said Suraj.

"And as for your place in the Team and your conduct during the tour," said the former opening batsman. "I think you lead the Team with distinction. You did as well as you could have in the situation."

"Thank you, Sir," said Suraj, his mind still trying to decipher what the President was getting to.

"And for that reason, we have decided to extend your term as Captain till the end of the Australian tour next year," said the President.

"You are not angry with me for my behaviour?" asked Suraj. "I mean, the ICC has started disciplinary proceedings against me."

"As I said, you did the best you could in the situation," he replied, "that being said, I would advise you to exercise caution from now on. You are the Captain of the Indian Cricket Team and people look up to you for guidance and inspiration."

"Does that mean that we must take stuff lying down?" asked Suraj.

"Absolutely not," said the President emphatically. "You must stand your ground, hit back at them when necessary."

"Okay," said Suraj.

The conversation between the President and Suraj went on for a few more minutes. After that, Suraj walked out of the rear entrance and saw that Aditi was standing against her car looking at her mobile phone.

"Hey," said Suraj.

"Hey you," said Aditi with a smile. "How was it?"

"Not bad actually," replied Suraj, "he was happy with my performance and has extended my term as Captain."

"That's great!" said Aditi and switched on the car.

"But I'm not sure I want to continue," said Suraj.

"Why not?" asked Aditi and switched off the car.

"I mean, I gave everything I had for this tour," said Suraj, "I worked harder than I ever have before and still I ended up losing. What if I can never lead the team to victory abroad?"

"Listen Suraj," said Aditi and placed her hand on his shoulder, "there is a verse in the Bhagavad Gita."

"Oh, I'm not interested in religion" replied Suraj.

"Just listen to what it says once," suggested Aditi, "and then decide whether you agree with it or not."

"Okay, what does it say?" asked Suraj.

"It says that you have control only over your actions and not on the fruits of your actions," explained Aditi. "All you can do is to give your best. The results are controlled by forces which are beyond our control."

"Okay, so does that mean that I should not expect results?" asked Suraj.

"No, in fact it says that you must have a goal," she said. "But if you do not achieve your goal, you must not succumb to inaction."

"Hmm," said Suraj, in deep thought.

"Do you understand what it means?" asked Aditi.

"I guess," replied Suraj.

"Do you know what you want to do?" asked Aditi starting the car.

"Yes," replied Suraj.

THE UGLY INDIANS

The loss to England made something in Suraj snap. He shed his skin of amiability and developed a harder edge to his personality. He no longer had friendly chats with the opposition Captain or players and resorted to sledging and abusing his opponents.

The first time when Suraj utilised this tactic was in the series against Sri Lanka. He would constantly bully and abuse the Sri Lankan players, which led to fines being imposed by the Match Referee. During the One Day Series against the Lankans, Suraj deposited his entire match fee with the match Referee in advance which led to a one-match ban being imposed on him.

The Indian media coined the name *"Captain Khadoos"* for Suraj. The behaviour of Suraj had not escaped the attention of the international cricketing media also, and they came up with the moniker *Ugly Indians* for the Indian Team.

"This Indian team is totally different from the docile teams of the past. We will not take shit from anyone anymore," Suraj said during one press conference. "I don't care if we are called *Ugly Indians* or anything else. All I care is going out in the field and winning."

"But why should you be abusive in the process?" asked one reporter.

"Next question please," said Suraj and looked away from the reporter.

"Suraj," said the reporter, "you have not answered my question."

"I have not answered your question, because it is a stupid question," responded Suraj rudely. "If you have something worthwhile to ask, I am here, otherwise I will go."

This lead to a sense of disquiet in the room full of reporters. No Indian Captain had ever treated them with such disdain.

"Nothing? I thought so," said Suraj and got up and left the press conference.

HOW DARE YOU!

England toured India for a five test match series in October 2026. Suraj used his influence to intimidate the curator at the venue of the first test to prepare a wicket which would turn square from Day One. His tactic worked as India won the first test comfortably. Using the power of his personality once more, Suraj convinced the curators for the remaining four Tests to prepare docile wickets. It was to ensure that England would not get back into the Series. Even though Aditi didn't agree with the tactics used by Suraj, she refrained from reprimanding him for the same. She felt that as Suraj was still hurting from the loss in England, this was his defence mechanism.

However, his tactics didn't work in the final test at the Wankhede Stadium in Mumbai as the curator prepared a competitive wicket. India went on the back foot from Day One itself and by the end of the Fourth Day, India was leading by 50 runs with only 3 wickets in hand. But with Suraj still batting, the crowd didn't lose hope.

On the fifth day, after a stubborn batting stint by Suraj, India managed to put up a lead of 150 runs for England to chase down with 30 overs left. On an ordinary day, chasing 150 runs in 30 overs was like a walk in the park, but on a crumbling wicket on the Fifth Day at the Wankhede Stadium, it was an uphill climb. Suraj and his team walked out onto the field knowing that the tide could turn against them. India had won the first Test of the five match series and Suraj desperately wanted to avoid defeat which would rob him of the opportunity to get revenge for the series loss in England.

After 20 overs, England had scored 98 runs for the loss of 2 wickets. They required only 52 runs in the balance 10 overs and that made Suraj a worried man. Meanwhile, in the pavilion, Aditi was nervously biting her nails along with the rest of the 33,000 strong crowd at the Wankhede Stadium.

Something has to be done, thought Suraj to himself.

"Kevin, come here," said Suraj and signaled to his newest left arm fast bowler.

"Yes?" said Kevin as he jogged along to Suraj.

"Suraj, you are taking up too much time," interjected the umpire.

"Yeah, this will take just a minute," replied Suraj to the umpire.

After the umpire had walked away, Suraj said to Kevin, "Kevin, take this ball and bowl wide on the leg side."

"Don't do it Kevin," warned the other senior members of the Indian Team who had gathered at the spot.

"That's not the right thing to do," said Kevin softly, who was afraid of Suraj and his formidable temper.

"Then would you rather lose this match?" snapped back Suraj.

"Listen, Suraj, I am not agreeing with this one bit," said one of the players.

"I don't care if you don't agree with it," said Suraj, "I will bowl half the overs myself."

"What's happening down there, Mr Singh?" asked Aditi as the meeting in the middle was taking too long.

"I have no clue," replied Mr. Singh, his face not betraying the nervousness he was feeling within.

He then called out the twelfth man and asked him to go out to see what was going on in the middle. When he heard about Suraj's plan, it shocked him.

"He wants to bowl wide outside the leg stump," said Mr. Singh, barely able to control his temper.

"Isn't that a little unsporting?" asked Aditi.

"A little? That's extremely unsporting!" replied Mr. Singh angrily.

After five more minutes of consultation, it was agreed that Kevin and Suraj would bowl the remaining ten overs after the rest of the bowlers refused to bowl according to their Captain's instructions. Suraj took the ball in his hand and walked towards the spot where he would start his run up. He bent down and picked up the marker, walked a further few feet and placed the marker down. Then using hand signals, he changed the field placements of the fielders. The batsmen, crowd and the umpires watched in bewilderment as Suraj placed almost all the fielders barring two, on the leg side. He then knelt down and started untying and tying his shoe laces.

The umpires instantly knew what was happening and reprimanded Suraj.

"Stop wasting time Suraj," said the umpire sternly.

"Sorry, Umps," replied Suraj, but continued fumbling with his shoe laces.

"I'll have to report you to the match referee, Suraj," said the other umpire.

"Sorry, Umps," repeated Suraj and finally managed to tie his shoe laces.

Realising that he had better get going, Suraj made the final adjustments to the field and ran in to bowl the ball. The ball pitched wide outside the leg stump. The batsman swung hard but could not make a connection. Suraj continued to do the same for the rest of the five balls.

After the last ball of the over was bowled, the English batsman who had faced the ball that over walked up to Suraj and said threateningly, "You better watch what you are doing, you sod!"

"Just mind your own fucking business," said Suraj, his voice loud enough so that the English batsman could hear but at the same time soft enough for the umpires not to notice.

"You think I'm stupid?" said the batsman and walked closer to Suraj, "Don't you think I know what you are doing?"

"Suck my cock, cunt," shot back Suraj abusively and walked away.

The two English batsmen then walked to the umpires and complained about the exchange of words.

"Come here, Suraj," said the umpire signaling to Suraj who was at mid-off.

"What?" said Suraj acting as if he had not heard the umpire's call.

"I said come here!" said the umpire again loudly.

Suraj then proceeded to walk towards the umpires at a leisurely pace.

"Come fast, don't waste our time!" said the other umpire.

"What happened?" asked Suraj, with an innocent expression on his face.

"First of all, you're wasting time," said the umpire.

"And secondly he abused me," interjected the English batsman.

"Don't teach me how to do my job," shot the umpire to the batsman, "keep your mouth shut."

"Sorry, Umps," said the English batsman and kept quiet.

"Did you use abusive language while addressing him?" asked the umpire pointing towards the English batsman.

"Abusive language? Absolutely not, Sir," said Suraj feigning innocence.

"He's lying! He called me a cunt!" said the batsman angrily.

"Shut up!" shouted the umpire and turned towards the batsman, "one more word from you and I'll report you as well to the Match Referee."

"Sorry, Umps," said the batsman.

"And don't call me Umps," said the umpire sternly, "call me umpire or Sir."

"Okay Sir," said the batsman.

"Suraj, are you saying that you did not using abusive language while addressing him?" asked the umpire.

"I did not Sir," reiterated Suraj as innocently as he could.

"Okay," said the umpire, "one more complaint against you and I will report you to the Match Referee."

"Whatever you think is right, Sir," said Suraj.

"Now get back to playing," said the umpire and the players walked towards their positions.

As they were walking Suraj's path crossed that of the English batsman.

"Fucking cocksucking cunt," said Suraj softly but loud enough for the Englishman to hear.

"Umpire he abused me again!" complained the English batsman to the umpire.

"Sir, now he is just wasting time," replied Suraj.

"That's enough!" said the umpire, "now get back to playing. We'll deal with your problems after the end of day's play."

"But-" said the English batsman.

"Enough! We've wasted enough time already," said the umpire, "now get back to your positions."

When the umpires looked away, Suraj sniggered at the English batsmen while making a lewd gesture.

This further angered the English batsmen. Fifteen precious minutes of play had been wasted and Suraj succeeded in breaking the concentration of the English batsmen.

Everything went according to plan for Suraj. He and Kevin bowled balls on the leg side for the remaining overs and stifled every possible opportunity of scoring for the Englishmen.

After eight overs had been bowled, the umpires converged and consulted each other all the while looking at a small piece of equipment.

"End of day's play," announced the umpires.

"Oh come on Sir, we can still play for a couple more overs," complained the English batsmen.

The English needed only 35 more runs from the allocated 3 overs which were remaining in the day and they thought that they had a good chance of pulling it off.

"Our decision is final," said the umpire. "The light is too bad for continuing play."

"Yessssss!!!" exclaimed Suraj running towards the stumps to uproot one of them.

But he was the only one celebrating. The rest of the Indian team was confused as to how they should react. While they were relieved that India had drawn the contentious Test match, the unsporting tactics used by their Captain muted their celebrations. Instead of exulting, they simply shook hands with each other and the opposition. Meanwhile the 33,000 strong crowd at the Wankhede Stadium had started booing and shouting slogans against Suraj.

A few hours later, Suraj sat in front of the television watching a comedy movie. He was completely exhausted from the day's play and was planning to sleep after a short while. While he knew deep down that his behavior that day was not appropriate, he had convinced himself that what he had done was right. He reasoned with himself that because the English had used unfair tactics during India's Tour to England, it was okay if he used similar tactics. His state of bliss was interrupted by the sound of the doorbell.

"Wonder who it is?" thought Suraj to himself as he walked towards the door.

His question was answered when he opened the door. It was Aditi. Disgusted by his behavior that day, Aditi did not meet Suraj after the end of day's play and instead had gone home.

"Hey! Where were you after stumps today?" asked Suraj coolly and leaned against the door.

Instead of an answer, Suraj felt a strong stinging on his left cheek as Aditi's right hand struck the portion below his left ear with a power which was completely disproportionate to her petite frame. Suraj stood there, stunned. He had never imagined in his wildest dreams that Aditi would do that.

"Think about what you did today, Suraj," said Aditi, her voice soft but firm.

Suraj gulped his saliva as he heard the words, his heart pounding hard inside his chest, a feeling of fear permeating every inch of his body.

"Do you know what they are calling you on the news, Suraj?" said Aditi, "They are calling you a thug. A thug, Suraj. That's what they are calling you."

Suraj opened his mouth to say something but no words came out.

"And you know what? I agree with them because what you did today was beyond disgusting," she said. "I never imagined that you could stoop so low in your life, Suraj. You have disappointed me. I am ashamed of having known you Suraj."

"But what about what the English did on our tour there?" asked Suraj softly.

"So does that justify what you did today?" said Aditi. "Just because they behaved badly, you think it's okay if you stoop down to their level? Didn't you ever think how it would affect the nation? Did you ever think how it would affect your teammates? Did you think how it would affect me? Do you know that I spoke to your teammates today? They have never experienced anything like this in their entire professional careers!"

Aditi stood there looking sternly at Suraj for a few moments without saying a single word.

"I've made my decision, Suraj," said Aditi. "We are done. Don't call me again and don't try to meet me again."

"But-" said Suraj.

"Just shut up Suraj! Shut the fuck up!" said Aditi loudly. "I am ashamed of having known a thug like you Suraj."

"Why don't you listen to my side of the story," pleaded Suraj.

"Goodbye, Suraj," said Aditi and turned around to walk away.

"Wait, Aditi!" said Suraj holding her hand.

"Let go of my hand, Suraj," said Aditi firmly.

"Please wait, come inside. Listen to what I have to say," pleaded Suraj.

"Let go of my hand!" said Aditi, this time louder. "Remember what I said. Don't try to contact me."

With that Aditi turned around and walked away. Suraj was left standing there outside his doorstep. He did not know what to think.

CHAMPIONS!!!

After much apologising, a few days later, Aditi started talking with Suraj. That was something for which Suraj was thankful for. He now needed somebody to talk to. He had just received a call from the BCCI that Mahesh Srivastava, another of India's fast bowlers had gotten injured in a practice session. The Final of the Champions Trophy was to take place and BCCI wanted to draft Suraj as a last minute replacement. He had received the call at around 11 am and the match was to start at 2:30 in the afternoon. The match was being held at the Wankhede Stadium, barely fifteen minutes away from Suraj's residence. The ban that Suraj had received after the final Test versus England meant that he would not be available for selection except if India reached the Finals. After he received the call stating their intent of drafting him as a replacement, Suraj told them that he would reply to them within fifteen minutes. He called up Aditi and told her about Mahesh's injury and about his decision to play the match, to which she agreed.

He called up the BCCI and confirmed that he would arrive at the stadium within the next half an hour and play.

South Africa won the toss and elected to bat. They posted 261 runs in 40 overs and were poised to go past the 300 run mark. It was then that Ajitesh, the stand-in Captain for the day walked up to Suraj and asked him what could be done to stem the flow of runs.

"Put a guy at third man," said Suraj, "half of their runs have come from there."

"Okay," he said, his face betraying the stress he was facing.

"What's the matter?" asked Suraj, realising that Ajitesh was under pressure.

"Can you take over for the next ten overs?" asked Ajitesh.

"Are you asking me to be the Captain for the next ten overs?" asked Suraj.

"Yes, I am," he said.

"Okay," said Suraj and cracked his knuckles.

For the last ten overs, Suraj took steps to stem the flow of runs with innovative field placements and brought himself on to bowl. He used all of his experience to bamboozle the South African batsmen with his variations and trickery. Noticing that the ball was stopping once it bounced on the pitch, Suraj instructed the other fast bowlers to bowl off and leg cutters. The plan worked. Runs were hard to come by for the Proteas and they finished their allotted 50 overs with a score of 297, a score which was no doubt daunting. But the entire Indian Team and supporters heaved a huge sigh of relief as it was much better to chase 297 than 350 or 400 which they would have had to had Suraj not intervened at the 40 over mark.

"Thanks Suraj," said Ajitesh.

"No problem buddy" replied Suraj with a smile. "But there is something I want from you."

"What?" asked Ajitesh.

"I want to open the batting," said Suraj.

"Okay, that's fine by me," replied Ajitesh.

"Thanks brother," replied Suraj.

The crowd at the Wankhede stadium is a peculiar one. They are a bunch of the most loud and passionate supporters in the game. But that day they did something which was done very few times before. They booed their own hometown player. Suraj had antagonised the entire crowd at the stadium during the last Test versus England when he decided to deliberately bowl wide in an attempt to stop England from scoring. And the crowd at the Wankhede that day did not stop themselves from heaping abuse on Suraj. Indian cricketers were known for their sportsmanship and the attitude of playing fair, so when Suraj brought his negative tactics to the fore, the crowd found it indefensible. And they let him know it in no uncertain terms.

The crowd immediately started booing and shouting slogans against Suraj when he walked out to bat at the start of the innings. But thankfully for the Indian team, Suraj was not affected much by all that. He understood the anger of the people and knew that had he been in their position, he would have done something similar.

Half an hour and five overs into the Indian innings, there was an increasing sense of impatience in the crowd. Suraj had played out 17 balls and had not scored a single run.

"Come on Suraj we don't have all fucking day!" shouted one member of the crowd.

It was the last ball of the over and the bowler bowled a ball which landed halfway down the pitch and bounced to about chest level of Suraj. However, instead of playing a pull shot or a hook shot, Suraj ducked into the ball. It was another dot ball. There was murmuring among members of the crowd and a while later they shouted in unison, "Fuck you Suraj Bhatkal!"

"Come on Suraj, do something," said the batsman at the other end to Suraj as they met at the end of the over.

"Yeah, give me the strike, I'll do something," replied Suraj.

At the first ball of the next over, the other batsman nudged the ball down to fine leg and took a single, thereby giving the strike to Suraj. The bowler then bowled a ball which landed at middle stump and moved away from Suraj. To this, Suraj just raised his hands above his head and let the ball go into the hands of the wicket keeper. The batsman at the other end kicked the ground in frustration. The match was slipping away from India's grasp as the required run rate was creeping towards six and a half runs per over.

"What the hell is he doing?" asked Mr. Singh to Aditi who was sitting with the rest of the team in the Dressing Room.

"I don't know," she replied, a frown on her face. "Whatever it is, I hope he does it fast."

After that delivery, Suraj took his mandatory walk away from the wicket towards the square leg umpire. When he walked back to the pitch, he started his ritual of tapping every part of his gear starting from his abdomen guard to his thigh pad and then his helmet. He then removed the strapping on his gloves and refastened it. After that, he closed his eyes and took three deep breaths.

The bowler ran towards the wicket and bowled a ball which landed at good length. Suraj danced down the track and swung his bat hard. The ball connected with the sweet spot of the bat and sailed into the third tier of the Wankhede Stadium. The crowd erupted in joy as the umpire raised his arms in the air to signal six runs. Suraj had finally opened his account. He hit two huge sixes off the remaining two balls of the over, one of which sailed outside the stadium. Now his score was 18 runs off 22 balls.

After that, Suraj did not play a single dot ball. He kept the South African fielders on their toes as he exploited gaps in the field and converted ones into twos. The South Africans realised that they were in for a titanic struggle. Suraj brought into action a plan which would make a huge dent in the armor of the Proteas without them realising it. With the coordination of the batsman at the other end, they would accumulate five runs off the first five balls. And then at the last ball, when all the fielders were relaxed after a relatively uneventful over, they would hit a four or a six, thus taking the total runs scored off the over to 9 or 11. And without anybody noticing, the required run rate slowly went below the five runs per over mark.

Suraj brought up his century in the 39th over. He raised his bat in the air acknowledging the rambunctious applause of the crowd. India went on to win the match in the 48th over with Suraj remaining not out at 156 runs off 124 balls. As they walked off the field, the South African players walked up to Suraj, shook his hand and congratulated him for a well-played innings. Suraj held back his tears as he saw every spectator in the stadium stand up and applaud him. He knew that the nation would not easily forgive him for his bad behavior in the match versus England. But this was a start – a good start.

BACK TO THE PRESENT

THE KNOCK

Suraj's mind was in a mess. He just could not stop thinking about Aditi and their kiss before he left for Australia. But did he have feelings for her? He did enjoy her company, he thought. Meanwhile, the hostile reception that the Indian Team got in Australia threw everyone off guard. Everybody from the Airport, Hotel and Ground Staff, gave them unfriendly stares as they walked about doing their business. Underprepared and slow wickets were given to the Indian Team to prepare, unlike the usual bouncy nature of the Australian wickets. This worried everyone especially because a majority of the team was touring Australia for the first time.

The tour games were also underwhelming, as reserve players were made to play against the Indians. There were reports in the notoriously hostile Australian media which said that the current Indian Team was the weakest to have landed on Australian shores. Thus, India came into the first test woefully underprepared and rudderless with their talismanic Captain battling his own demons.

"Cap!" said a voice to his right.

What should I do? How can I get out of this mess, thought Suraj to himself.

"Cap!" said the voice again.

"Yeah? What?" said Suraj sounding startled.

"What should I do?" asked the bowler, Kevin.

"What do you mean?" asked Suraj.

"He's still smashing the hell out of me, Cap!" said Kevin.

"Yeah," said Suraj and became silent.

"So what should I do?" asked Kevin again after Suraj did not say anything for a while.

"Bowl the ball in the channel," instructed Suraj.

"The channel?" he asked a confused expression on his face.

"Yeah, the channel, outside the off stump," said Suraj. "The corridor of uncertainty."

"Oh, okay," replied Kevin, not sounding entirely convinced. "Anything else?"

"Yeah, pray that he fucks up," said Suraj under his breath.

But Suraj's plan did not work. The Australians piled on a mammoth 679 runs in just one and a half days. When India went on to bat, they lost 3 wickets quickly. As Suraj walked in to bat, his heart was beating fast with fear permeating every inch of his body. He struggled to connect bat to ball. Even though he was a notoriously slow starter, this was different. Every time he would struggle to score, Suraj would use the power of concentration to wade through the turbulent waters. But now, the cricket pitch was the last place he wanted to be. How he hoped and wished that he could be back in India with Aditi to spend time with her. He was barely concentrating when the bowler went to the start of his run up and started running towards Suraj to bowl the next delivery. It pitched around midway, bounced viciously and whizzed past his helmet. The bowler then walked towards Suraj, stood barely a foot away and gave him the choicest of abuses. That rattled Suraj even more.

"Concentrate dammit!" he said to himself.

He tried to clear his mind by taking a deep breath. He decided to himself that if the next ball was a bouncer like the previous one, he would hook it, hoping that a good connection to the bat would get him back into the groove.

Suraj took his stance and waited for the bowler to bowl the ball. As expected, it was a bouncer. Suraj rocked on to his back foot and swung his bat to execute a hook shot. But instead of making a connection with the bat, the ball bounced more than expected and hit Suraj just below the ear on the unprotected part of his head. He bent down for a moment and then fell to the ground.

Back in India, Aditi had been glued to the television. She was nervous as she watched Suraj struggling to play. Fear permeated her body as she saw the ball hit Suraj's ear and saw Suraj collapse to the ground.

"Oh God!" she exclaimed loudly.

"What happened, dear?" asked her father who was reading the newspaper.

"Suraj got hit, papa," said a panicked Aditi.

Her father sat next to her and they watched replays of the ball which had felled the Indian Captain. Medical personnel had arrived on the field with their equipment to examine Suraj, who lay on the ground unconscious.

"He's not moving papa," said Aditi frantically.

"Don't worry dear," said her father putting an arm around her, trying to calm her down. "I'm sure he'll be fine."

The Medical team spent close to ten minutes on the field examining Suraj. Suraj, who did not respond to their treatment, was placed on a stretcher and was taken off the field.

A few hours later, Aditi was pacing nervously in the living room. Her father had decided not to go to the clinic that day. News updates on Suraj were coming in thick and fast. But she gasped when she saw the next headline which said "Suraj Bhatkal is in a coma and has internal bleeding."

"He's what?" said Aditi's father on the phone. He was talking to the doctor of the Indian Cricket Team.

"Papa, he's in a coma," said Aditi with tears in her eyes, her entire body shaking.

"He's fine dear," said her father reassuringly after hanging up.

"But he's in a coma," said Aditi frantically.

"He's in a medically-induced coma," replied her father.

"And what about the internal bleeding?" asked Aditi, feeling slightly relieved.

"There is bound to be some swelling and bleeding after being hit by a cricket ball right?" said her father. "But it's nothing serious. The ball did not hit any critical part. They have put him in a coma as a precaution."

"Okay," said Aditi feeling her pulse slowing down a little.

The doctors kept Suraj in a medically-induced coma for three whole days after which they revived him. When he woke up, he saw a woman sitting beside him on the bed.

"Oh my God, you're here!" said Suraj, not believing his eyes. The woman was Aditi, who had gotten on the first available flight to Australia.

"Thank God you are okay, I was so worried," she said and caught him in a tight embrace.

"Why are you here? What about your clinic?" asked Suraj, still surprised.

"Oh, to hell with the clinic," said Aditi, still maintaining a tight grip on Suraj, "my father can manage without me for a few days."

After a while, they let go of each other. Aditi sat on the bed and took Suraj's hand into hers.

"Uh, I wanted to tell you something," said Aditi.

"I too wanted to tell you something," said Suraj.

"You go first," she said.

"No you say first," he said.

"Just tell me what you have to say you dumbass," she said with a chuckle.

"Okay," said Suraj and took a deep breath. "I have thought about what you said before I left, and I have an answer for you."

"Now is not the time to talk about that Suraj," said Aditi gently, "you have too many things on your mind now."

"But-" started Suraj.

"Not now dear," said Aditi and gently ran her hand through his hair.

"Okay," said Suraj, "whatever you say."

"So how badly did we lose?" asked Suraj after a while.

"We lost badly, that's all you need to know," replied Aditi.

"Hmm," said Suraj, feeling a sense of disappointment.

"Let's not think about that now dear," said Aditi reassuringly, "you had better go to sleep. You need to rest."

THE LONG ROAD BACK

It had been a couple of days since Suraj had been discharged from the hospital. The next Test was to start in a week's time. The doctors had told Suraj that he could start training again. Suraj did go back to training, but his mind was not in the right place. The memories of the blow he had received still haunted him. He started becoming aloof and was not taking part in Team discussions. This did not escape the attention of Mr. Singh. He called Aditi one day and had a talk with her about Suraj.

"Is he saying anything to you?" asked Mr. Singh.

"He has not said anything," replied Aditi. "But he was never one to talk much anyways."

"He is still on medication right?" he asked.

"Yes," she replied, "We had increased the dose a couple of months ago."

"What can we do?" asked the Coach, "The team's morale is in shambles; we were thrashed in the First Test and the next Test is barely a week away. We need Suraj to get back to his best."

"Yeah, I know," replied Aditi, deep in thought.

They spent the next few moments in silence, both of them racking their brains for a solution.

"I have an idea," said Aditi after a while, breaking the silence.

"What is it?" asked the Coach.

"Suraj responds well when he is challenged," she said.

"So what do you have in mind?" he asked.

Aditi leaned forward and told the coach what was on her mind.

At the Adelaide Oval, Suraj had finished jogging five laps of the stadium. He then went to the nets and bowled for an hour. After that, he padded up and decided to bat for a while. Seeing that Suraj was in the nets batting, Mr. Singh called Zohar, the Bowling Coach and said something in his ear.

Suraj adjusted his gear and looked around the ground. He saw that Aditi was standing next to Mr. Singh. Even though she followed all his matches religiously, she had never attended a nets session before. Zohar went up to Kevin and gave him some instructions.

Suraj then took his stance and waited for Kevin to bowl. The ball pitched halfway, bounced viciously and missed Suraj's helmet by a whisker.

"What the fuck!" exclaimed Suraj angrily and walked threateningly towards Kevin.

It was an unspoken rule that during nets sessions bowlers would not bowl bouncers at the batsmen.

"Sorry, Zohar bhai told me to do so" replied Kevin softly pointing at the Bowling Coach.

"What the fuck man! Why did you tell him to bowl bouncers at me?" shouted Suraj walking towards Zohar.

"What's the matter? You afraid?" he taunted.

"Like hell I am!" replied Suraj. "Bring it on! I'll spank his ass black and blue today!"

Half an hour later, after Suraj effortlessly navigated Kevin's hostile bowling, Mr. Singh looked at Aditi with a grin.

"He's back," said the Coach.

"Yep!" replied Aditi, a satisfied smile on her face.

THE NOSE JOB

In the Second Test, India fought back and were more competitive. Suraj's captaincy was instrumental in this performance. Australia, after a late flurry by the lower order, set India a Target of 358 runs. The openers gave India a good start, scoring 115 runs at a brisk pace by the end of Day 4. But soon after resumption of play on Day 5, India lost 4 quick wickets. India was precariously placed at 125 for the loss of 4 wickets and with 233 runs still left to win. Suraj, who had walked in after the loss of the third wicket, was batting in a desperate attempt to keep his Team in the game. However, the going was very tough. The Australian bowlers had sensed a weakness and they pounced immediately, taking advantage of the vulnerability of the Indians.

Roughly an hour later, Suraj's score had not changed. The strong Australian bowling attack with four pacemen had tightened the screws and the attacking field placements made scoring close to impossible.

When Suraj took strike his score was at 13 runs off 158 balls. The fastest of the four Australian bowlers started taking his long run up and delivered a ball which landed halfway down the pitch and bounced viciously. Suraj raised his bat to around his face in an attempt to fend off the ball, but his reflexes were not fast enough. The ball bowled at an astonishing speed of 156 kilometers per hour, broke through the visor of Suraj's helmet and hit him right between the eyes.

Suraj immediately fell to the ground in a heap. Rizwan, the batsman at the other end, the Australian players and both the umpires converged at the scene.

"Cap, are you all right?" asked Rizwan frantically, urgency in his voice.

"Suraj," said one of the umpires, "say something."

"Call the Doctor fast!" said Rizwan and signaled to the Dressing Room.

The medical unit of the Indian Cricket Team rushed onto the field within a matter of seconds. Dr. Irani the portly, overweight Doctor of the Indian Team got down to his knees to assess the damage. It was a grotesque scene. The ball had struck the top of the nose and blood was gushing out of it. Suraj himself half conscious was barely aware of what was happening around him. Dr. Irani removed a tube containing a liquid and placed it in Suraj's nostrils. When Suraj took one breath of the liquid, he immediately sat up straight.

"Oh fuck!" said Suraj, suddenly fully conscious and feeling the full effect of the pain.

"Suraj, can you see me?" asked Dr. Irani.

"Fuck! My nose hurts!" replied Suraj, with tears of agony gushing from his eyes.

"Suraj, look at me," said Dr. Irani and turned Suraj's head towards him.

"Huh?" said Suraj, his eyes barely open.

"I'll put some cotton in your nose to stop the bleeding," said Dr. Irani, "and it will hurt."

"Oh fuck man! Fuck! Fuck! Fuck!" exclaimed Suraj as Dr. Irani put the pieces of cotton inside his nose.

About 20 minutes later, Suraj was fully lucid, even though the pain had not reduced. The bleeding had now stopped. Suraj walked around, holding the pieces of cotton to his nose, as both the teams took a breather.

Mr. Singh came onto the field and spoke to Dr. Irani to understand the extent of the damage.

"He has broken his nose," said Dr. Irani.

"Are you sure?" asked the Coach.

"Obviously I'm sure! I'm a Doctor dammit, I know a broken nose when I see it," replied Dr. Irani irritably.

"Okay, so what now?" asked Mr. Singh.

"I will have to admit him into a hospital," said Dr. Irani, "he has lost a lot of blood."

"I'm not going anywhere," said a voice behind them.

"What?" said Dr. Irani, turning around to see Suraj behind them.

"I'm not going to the hospital," said Suraj, who was tilting his head backwards and holding the pieces of cotton in his nostrils.

"But you've broken your nose Suraj!" said Dr. Irani, "And you've lost a lot of blood!"

"I don't give a flying fuck," replied Suraj, determination in his voice, "I'm playing."

"But Suraj"- started the Coach.

"I know what you are going to say, boss," said Suraj interrupting Mr. Singh, "but I've made up my mind. I've got a job to do and a broken nose is not going to stop me from doing it."

"But"- said Dr. Irani.

"There are no ifs and buts, Dr. Irani," said Suraj defiantly, "do whatever is required right here. I'm not leaving the field."

"What can be done?" asked the Coach to Dr. Irani.

"First of all I'll have to set his nose into place," replied Dr. Irani, "that itself is a big task."

"And then?" asked Mr. Singh.

"I'll have to put a lot of stuffing into his nose to properly stop the bleeding," said Dr. Irani.

"So you can do it right?" asked the Coach.

"I mean I can do it," said Dr. Irani tentatively, shrugging his shoulders.

"What's the problem? Do it!" said the Coach.

"It's going to hurt like hell," whispered Dr. Irani.

"I can still hear you!" said Suraj from behind them.

"Okay, Suraj," said the Coach and walked upto him. "Dr. Irani will put your nose into place and put some stuffing into it to stop the bleeding."

"Okay," replied Suraj, "but will I be able to play?"

"Suraj, why don't you reconsider your decision?" asked Mr. Singh, hoping that Suraj would change his mind. "We can take you to a hospital and everything can be done there."

"Nothing doing boss, I'm staying right here," replied Suraj. "What if I go off the field and we lose the remaining wickets and lose the match? What happens then? We'd have lost the chance to win the series!"

"Listen Suraj, winning the series is the last thing on my mind now," said the Coach, "what I care about right now is your well being."

"Well then your priorities are wrong," snapped back Suraj. "I'm not changing my mind. Do whatever stuff you want to do on my nose right here. I don't care if it hurts."

"Okay then, you have left me with no choice," said Dr.

Irani with a shrug, "come here."

Suraj walked up to him and Dr. Irani, whose white gloves were stained with blood, placed his hands on Suraj's nose.

"Now take a deep breath," said Dr. Irani, "and count to three."

"Okay," said Suraj and took a deep breath. "One, two. Oh fuck! Fuck! Motherfucker!"

"Didn't I say it would hurt?" said Dr. Irani with a shrug.

"But you also said that you would do it at the count of three!" said Suraj, feeling a fresh wave of excruciating pain.

"No I didn't," replied Dr. Irani, "I just told you to count upto three. I never said that I would fix your nose at the count of three."

"Smartass," said Suraj softly and grimaced.

THE FIRST CENTURY

With his nose stuffed to the brim, Suraj continued batting. The Australian bowlers, reinvigorated after the break, had found another gear and had cranked up the pace by a notch or two. But now, Suraj's mindset was different. He knew that going on the offensive would not reap rewards. So, he decided to play the waiting game. He blocked or left every delivery that he faced and instructed Rizwan at the other end to also do the same. They agreed that time was on their side and that if they played out that tough spell, the Australian bowlers would eventually tire and bowl loose deliveries which they could capitalise on.

It took some time, but Suraj's plan worked. As predicted, the Australian bowlers became tired and their line and length wavered. Suraj and Rizwan seized the opportunity and finally the scoring rate went up.

Suraj became so engrossed in the task on hand that he did not notice when he crossed the half century mark and also when his nose started bleeding.

He hit the fastest of the four Australian bowlers for a six right over his head. The bowler then walked up to Suraj and said, "Your nose is bleeding, mate."

"Yeah, yeah, just do your fucking job," shot back Suraj.

"I'm serious mate, your nose is bleeding," said the bowler, "call the Doctor."

Suraj then looked down and saw that blood was indeed pouring out of his nose. The umpire signaled the Indian dressing room and called for the team Doctor.

"Make it quick," said Suraj when Dr. Irani came onto the field with his medical kit, "don't want the Aussies to have a rest."

When Suraj started batting, he controlled the tempo of the game by taking quick ones and twos. This frustrated the Australians and they resorted to their time tested strategy of sledging, or what they called *mental disintegration*. But Suraj was ready for it and when he gave it back to them in equal measure, the Aussies got rattled.

Slowly and steadily, the Indians inched towards the target set by the Australians. Suraj, now deep in the "Zone", didn't even realise that he has scored a century a couple of hours later. The whole crowd made up mostly of Australians, stood up and applauded Suraj for a minute straight.

"Why are they clapping?" asked Suraj, when he saw that the clapping had not subsided.

"You've scored a century, Cap!" replied Rizwan excitedly.

"Oh, okay," replied Suraj, casually.

"Raise your bat and acknowledge them, Cap!" said Rizwan.

"Oh, yes," said Suraj and raised his bat to acknowledge the applause of the crowd.

When they were within 20 runs of winning, they lost another wicket.

"Sorry I couldn't hang around, Cap," said a dejected Rizwan before he left for the pavilion.

"It's okay Riz," replied Suraj, giving a pat on his back, "you've done your bit. Thanks."

About 15 minutes later, India need only 3 runs to win when the Australians started complaining about bad light, as they want play to stop for the day.

"Nothing doing," said one of the umpires, looking right through the excuse of the fielding side, "they deserve to win. I will not call off play now."

The Australians set attacking fields, in an attempt to stem the flow of runs. But they were unsuccessful as Suraj hit one ball straight into the crowd. He raised his arms in triumph as India completed a famous win. Suraj was named Man of the Match, but he gave the post match presentation a miss and asked Rizwan to attend it in his place.

ESCAPE TO VICTORY

Having gotten inspiration from their win in the Second Test, India found a second life and pushed the Australians to the brink of defeat in the Third Test at Perth. Australia managed to avoid defeat in the Third Test because rain came to their rescue. The two teams then travelled to Sydney for the final test. Memories of the England Tour came back to Suraj's mind, but a session with Aditi convinced him to use it as inspiration instead of getting bogged down by it.

However, something else was bothering Suraj. He was experiencing a nagging pain in his right shoulder and after having a scan; it was revealed that there was a tear in the rotator cuff. The Doctor advised Suraj to miss the final Test, to prevent further damage from being done, but Suraj refused. His will to win was much greater than the pain he was feeling. The Doctor then told him that he could play only on the condition that he would limit his bowling and throw balls underarm while fielding. He warned Suraj that if he would not do as told; the injury would worsen and he would require surgery and a lengthy recovery period. Suraj, decided to play the Final Test after taking pain-killers that would reduce the intensity of pain. It was also decided that the rest of the team should not be made aware of his injury, lest it distract them.

India dominated the proceedings in the final test and on the final Day, Australia needed 189 runs with 5 wickets in hand. The Indians sensed an opportunity and went for the kill. However, Suraj didn't get himself on to bowl as the discomfort in his shoulder had gone up a notch. India kept on taking wickets at regular intervals, but the progress was slow as the Australian batsmen knuckled down and uncharacteristically played for a draw.

Going into the last hour, India needed only 2 wickets to win, but the stubborn resistance offered by the Aussie batsmen frustrated the Indians.

Suraj, ignoring the advice of the Doctor, decided to bowl. He managed to pick up a wicket, but when he was fielding, he stopped a ball by diving to his right. This caused further damage to his already injured right shoulder and he had to leave the field in tears. He knew that he could not play any further part in the match.

Suraj sat in the Dressing Room, inconsolable, with Aditi by his side.

"I wonder who it is," said Aditi as she heard her mobile ring and picked it up.

"Aditi, it's me, Sanjeev," said the voice at the other end, "Suraj's father."

"Oh yes, uncle," replies Aditi, caught by surprise by the unexpected call.

"May I have a word with Suraj, please?" asked Sanjeev softly.

"He wants to talk to you," said Aditi to Suraj.

"Okay, give it to me," said Suraj and took the mobile from her hand.

"Hello son," said Sanjeev.

"Hello Papa," replied Suraj.

There was an awkward silence for a few moments after which Sanjeev said, "Suraj, I want to tell you something. I have always been proud of you. I think that you are amazing at what you do. I haven't told you this earlier because I thought that it would make you complacent."

"Thanks Papa," replied Suraj, feeling a lump in his throat.

"What are you doing now?" he asked.

"I'm in the Dressing room," said Suraj, "I hurt my shoulder again."

"Suraj, will you do something for me?" asked Sanjeev.

"Sure, Papa," he replied.

"Go out on the field and show those bastards who is the boss!" said Sanjeev forcefully.

"Yes, Papa," replied Suraj. "I love you Papa."

"Love you too dear," replied Sanjeev. "Now go out there and smash them!"

Suraj felt energy run through his body. He knew exactly what he had to do.

"Do you have a sling?" he asked and got up.

"A sling? Why would you want a sling?" asked Aditi.

"I want to go out on the field," replied Suraj.

"No Suraj dear, you have done enough," said Aditi and tried to make Suraj sit down.

"I'm not going to listen to you now, Aditi," said Suraj. "Find me a sling!"

With some help from Dr. Irani, Suraj put his injured right arm in a sling and walked out on to the field, much to the bewilderment of the 46,000 spectators in the Sydney Cricket Ground.

Suraj stood at his customary position of mid-off and handed the ball to Kevin.

"Get me a wicket," said Suraj, "I don't care how you do it. Set the field you want."

Kevin bowled the over of his life, but was unable to get the last Australian batsman out.

Suraj switched his bowlers around hoping to get the final breakthrough, but to no avail. When it was announced by the umpires that the last over of the day would be bowled, Suraj called Kevin and asked him to bowl the last over.

The crowd held their breath as Kevin took his long run up and bowled the first five deliveries. However, he was unable to get the batsman out.

"Sorry, Cap," said Kevin, dejectedly.

"Don't worry, there's one final ball left," replied Suraj, "anything can happen. I have full faith in you."

Buoyed by the faith placed in him by his Captain, Kevin bowled a delivery on which the batsman played a pull shot, intending to dispatch it to the boundary. However, instead of hitting the sweet spot of the bat, the ball went high up in the air.

"Mine!" shouted Suraj.

Suraj ran towards the ball, threw his left hand out and felt the ball land smack into his palm. After a moment, he threw the ball in the air in joy as he realised that India had won the Match and the Series! The Australian batsman fell to the ground in despair. Suraj, before celebrating with his team, walked up to the two Australian players on the field and shook hands with them.

During the Presentation Ceremony, the Australian Captain was gracious in defeat and complimented Suraj on his tenacity and attitude. He felt that *Suraj was good enough to be an Australian.*

On the flight back to India, Suraj who was travelling with Aditi told her that he also had feelings for her.

When they got off at Mumbai International Airport, they saw that Suraj's father was waiting to receive them. Suraj walked up to his father tentatively.

"Come here my son!" said Sanjeev, opening his arms.

Suraj hugged him for the first time in many years.

"I'm sorry that I was so harsh on you in the past, Suraj," said Sanjeev, with tears in his eyes.

"No need to say sorry for anything, Papa," replied Suraj, maintaining a tight grip on his father.

EPILOGUE – 20 YEARS LATER

Suraj entered his home after his customary morning walk. As he walked inside, he heard his cell phone ringing.

"Hello," he said as he picked up the phone.

"Hello, Mr. Bhatkal?" said the voice at the other end.

"Yes," he replied.

"I am speaking on behalf of the President of the BCCI," said the lady.

"Okay," replied Suraj.

"The President would like to meet you today" she asked.

"At what time should I come?" he asked.

"How about lunchtime?" suggested the lady.

"Okay, I'll be there, but what is this about?" he asked.

"Uh, the President would like to tell you himself Sir," she said.

"Okay, so I'll be there at one," said Suraj.

"Thank you, Sir," said the lady, "have a nice day."

"You too," said Suraj and put the phone down.

Suraj wondered what the President of the BCCI would like to say to him. After his retirement from cricket, he did not have any contact with the top cricket administration body of the country. His mind was still racing as he picked up his phone and told his colleague that he would be taking the day off.

A few hours later, Suraj sat in the reception area outside the office of the President of the BCCI. The memories of sitting in the same spot about twenty years ago were fresh in his mind. He wondered what the new President of the BCCI had in mind.

"Come in, Suraj," said the President of the BCCI, a former left handed opening batsman.

"Hello, Sir," said Suraj and shook his hand.

"Please have a seat," he said, "will you have something? Tea or coffee?"

"Tea, Sir," replied Suraj.

"You must be wondering what this is about?" asked the President getting straight to the point.

"Yes, you've got my attention," replied Suraj.

"I want your opinion on something," said the President. "What qualities must a good coach have?"

"Oh. I think he must be like a friend to the team members." said Suraj after a while, initially stumped by the question.

"So he should be friendly," he said.

"Yes, but he must also be stern. I mean the players must not take him for a ride or something," added Suraj.

"Anything else?" asked the President, "like is it necessary for him to be a good technician? As in, should he be responsible for getting the technique of the batsmen and bowlers correct?"

"I don't think it is a necessity," said Suraj honestly, "I think it is better if there are good batting or bowling Coaches in the team to support the Head Coach."

"Absolutely," said the President leaning forward, "so that there is not much stress on the one person right?"

"Yes," replied Suraj, wondering where the conversation was headed.

"Suraj, what are you up to these days?" asked the President, "I heard you are working in a company."

"Yes," replied Suraj.

"In what designation?" he asked.

"As Head of Administration," replied Suraj.

"Is it something that interests you?" he asked, "I mean, do you like what you do?"

"It's okay. I mean I have good and bad days," replied the former all rounder.

"Do you miss cricket?" asked the President.

"Yes, sometimes I do," he replied.

"I heard that you are coaching your son's school cricket team," said the former opening batsman.

"Yes, I help them out sometimes," replied Suraj.

"Okay, Suraj, I think we have had enough of small talk. The real reason why I wanted you to come meet me today is because of this," said the President and handed a thin file to Suraj.

When Suraj opened the file and looked at it, he was rendered speechless.

"Sir, are you sure you have made the right choice?" asked Suraj, still trying to process the things written on the paper in front of him.

"I am one hundred percent sure," said the President.

Later that evening, Suraj was watching the news when Aditi came in.

"You're home early," she said and put her bag down.

"I was called to Headquarters today," replied Suraj.

"But don't you always go there" she asked as she sat down next to him.

"Not that Headquarters, the other one," said Suraj with a grin.

"You mean BCCI Headquarters?" she asked excitedly. "What did they want?"

"This," said Suraj and handed over a thin file to his wife.

"What's this?" she asked.

"Read it," he said.

"They want to make you Coach?" she said excitedly after she went through the document.

"Yes," replied Suraj.

"As in, Head Coach of the Indian Cricket Team?" she asked.

"Yes," he replied.

"That's amazing!" she said and hugged her husband.

"Yeah," said Suraj softly.

"Now don't tell me that you refused the offer," she said.

"I didn't, I said that I will think about it," replied Suraj.

"What? Why?" she asked.

"I have never coached a team dear," explained Suraj.

"But I think you'll be awesome," she said and snuggled up next to him.

"You think so?" he asked, turning to her.

"Obviously!" she said.

"But why?" he asked.

"Don't know, I just have a feeling you'll do a great job," she said.

"Okay," he said.

"So will you at least think about it?" asked his wife.

"Okay, but first let me talk to Kedar tomorrow," replied Suraj.

The next morning, Suraj walked through entrance of his office building and went to meet Kedar Shetty, the Chief of the Administration Department. After a bit of small talk, Kedar, about ten years older than Suraj, got to the point.

"So what did you want to talk to me about Suraj?" he asked.

"I had taken leave yesterday for some urgent work," said Suraj.

"Yes, I know," replied Kedar, "but what does that have to do with what you want to talk about?"

"I was called to BCCI Headquarters," said Suraj.

"Oh, okay," replied Suraj's boss. "What did they want?"

"They want to make me the Head Coach of the Indian Cricket team," he said.

Kedar became quiet for a few moments trying to process the information.

"Oh, wow!" he said finally.

"Yes, I know," replied Suraj with a chuckle, "it was my response as well."

"So what have you thought?" asked Kedar.

"I thought I should discuss it with you first," said Suraj.

"What did Aditi say?" asked Kedar.

"She told me to at least consider it," replied Suraj.

"Hmm," murmured Kedar, in deep thought.

"Actually I don't know what to do," said Suraj, "I have never coached a cricket Team."

"But don't you coach your son's team?" asked Kedar.

"Yeah, but that's different," said Suraj. "They are just kids."

"I think that if you can coach a bunch of rowdy teenagers you can coach anybody," said Kedar with a small laugh. "But in all seriousness, what does your gut say?"

"I don't know," said Suraj looking confused. "One part of me says that I should go for it. But the other says that I must not because I don't have any experience of serious coaching. And it would also mean that I must stay away from Aditi and the kids."

They spent the next few moments in silence with both of them in deep thought.

"Listen Suraj," said Kedar breaking the silence. "I think you should take the job. I strongly believe that you will be the best person to coach the Indian Cricket Team."

"Okay," replied Suraj, "can you give me a reason?"

"See, there are a lot of points in your favour," said Kedar. "Firstly, you are an amazing teacher. You have endless patience. The way you have taught your assistant her job has left not only me but everybody else astounded. She has been in the organisation for less than a year and yet she can handle all the work. I think a lot of the credit has to go to you."

"Thanks, you're being very kind," said Suraj modestly.

"Oh come on Suraj, you know that I never praise anybody until and unless they really deserve it," said Kedar.

"Okay, what else?" asked Suraj.

"You have been the greatest cricketer India has produced since the Little Master himself. Do you know that people had stopped watching cricket for more than a decade when you started playing the game? I think it was the England Tour that rejuvenated that interest in the game and all that was because of you. I know you don't believe in God and all that, but I believe that you are a Godsend for this team. The team will benefit immensely from your presence alone," said Kedar.

"Hmm," said Suraj, processing the pros and cons in his mind.

"What do you think?" asked Kedar after a while.

"I'll sleep over it for a couple of days and evaluate after that," said Suraj.

"Sounds good," said Kedar.

Later that evening Suraj had a long discussion with Aditi about the pros and cons of taking the job as India's Coach.

"I'll take the job," said Suraj, a sense of finality in his voice.

A few days later, Suraj tendered his resignation letter at his office.

THE FIRST DAY ON THE JOB

Suraj stood at the edge of the HPCA Cricket Stadium at Dharamshala, awestruck with the beauty of its backdrop. Touching the ground in respect, he slowly walked towards the pitch. Once there, he bent down and inspected the pitch. There was a thick layer of grass on it just as he had requested. A few moments later, the players started walking out on to the ground and made their way towards Suraj.

After all the players had assembled onto the ground, Suraj cleared his throat.

"Let us begin," he said, with a smile.

About the Author

A full-time Finance Professional, Arjun Hemmady has been interested in writing since an early age. He has written various articles on topics such as driving and sports and the current socio-political scenario in India. The next step in his literary journey was definitely then to write a novel. He published his first novel at the age of 26, titled "You Raise Me Up" in November 2015. When not working, Arjun likes to cook, read, drive and watch movies and sports.

Write to Arjun at - arjunhemmady@gmail.com

facebook.com/arjunhemmady

instagram/arjunhemmady

